Bf 109D/E Aces 1939–41

SERIES EDITOR: TONY HOLMES

OSPREY AIRCRAFT OF THE ACES® • 11

Bf 109D/E Aces 1939–41

John Weal

OSPREY
PUBLISHING

Front cover
Sensing that his 56th kill is just moments away, then ranking *Jagdwaffe* ace Major Helmut Wick turns in behind the already smoking Spitfire I R6631 of No 609 'West Riding' Sqn's Plt Off Paul A Baillon as the pair race over The Needles at the western end of the Isle of Wight on the afternoon of 28 November 1940. Having power dived into the Auxiliary squadron from a superior height over the Solent, the *Gruppenkommandeur* of I./JG 2 had quickly singled out the hapless Baillon and hit his Spitfire hard with a well aimed burst of cannon and machine gun fire from Bf 109E-4 Wk-Nr 5344 – Wick's favoured mount throughout the later months of 1940.

Canadian ace Plt Off Keith A Ogilvie was part of the No 609 Sqn formation engaged by I./JG 2, and he described the attack as follows; 'I was Yellow 3 and was weaving merrily behind, keeping an eagle eye above, when I caught a glimpse of three "yellow noses" in my mirror. They were obviously crack pilots by their tight formation and strategy. I gave the warning and dove as the centre Johnny opened fire on me, and was speeded on my way by a cannon shot up the fuselage and a second through my prop.'

Despite having had his aircraft superficially damaged in the initial attack, Ogilvie shook off his assailants and saw Plt Off Baillon bail out of his stricken Spitfire about 20 miles south of Bournemouth. He followed his squadronmate's progress down into the water, but was dismayed to see the pilot display no signs of life whilst floating beneath the perfectly deployed parachute. Baillon's body was later washed up on the Normandy coast. His conqueror, meanwhile, had little time to celebrate his latest kill, for Wick in turn fell victim to No 609 Sqn's leading ace, Flt Lt John C Dundas, less than five minutes later

First published in Great Britain in 1996 by Osprey Publishing, Elms Court, Chapel Way, Botley, Oxford, OX 2 9 LP, United Kingdom.
Email: info@ospreypublishing.com

© 1996 Osprey Publishing
© 1996 Aerospace Publishing Colour Side-views

CIP Data for this publication is available from the British Library
ISBN-10 : 1-85532-487-3
ISBN-13 : 978-1-85532-487-9
Edited by Tony Holmes
Page design by TT Designs, T & S Truscott

Weal, John

Bf 109D/E aces, 1939-1941 / John Weal   ers
                                                          5 5
                              940.
                                544   Mason, Michael Payne and
1862429   ial photographs.

Editor's Note
To make this best-selling series as authoritative as possible, the editor would be extremely interesed in hearing from any individual who may have relevant photographs, documentation or first-hand experiences relating to the elite pilots, and their aircraft, of the various theatres of war. Any materials used will be fully credited to its original source. Please write to Tony Holmes, 16 Sandilands, Chipstead, Sevenoaks, Kent, TN13 2SP.

FOR A CATALOGUE OF ALL BOOKS PUBLISHED BY OSPREY PLEASE CONTACT:
NORTH AMERICA
Osprey Direct, C/o Random House Distribution Center, 400 Hahn Road, Westminster, MD 21157
E-mail: info@ospreydirect.com

ALL OTHER REGIONS
Osprey Direct UK, P.O. Box 140, Wellingborough, Northants, NN8 2FA, UK
E-mail: info@ospreydirect.co.uk

www.ospreypublishing.com

CONTENTS

BIRTH OF THE BLITZKRIEG

Bf 109 UNITS IN CENTRAL AND EASTERN GERMANY, 1/9/39

Luftflottenkommando 1 (North-East) HQ: Stettin/Pommerania

		Base	Type	Est-Serv
1. Fliegerdivision (Schönfeld/Crössinsee)				
I.(J)/LG 2	Hptm Hanns Trübenbach	Malzkow, Lottin	Bf 109E	42-33
JGr.101 (II./ZG 1)	Maj Reichardt	Lichtenau	Bf 109E	48-48
5.(J)/TrGr.186	Oblt Gerhard Kadow	Stolp, Brüsterort	Bf 109B/E	23-23
6.(J)/TrGr.186	Hptm Heinrich Seeliger	Stolp, Brüsterort	Bf 109B/E	23-23
Luftgaukommando I (Königsberg/East Prussia)				
I./JG 1	Maj Bernhard Woldenga	Gutenfeld	Bf 109E	46-46
I./JG 21	Hptm Martin Mettig	Gutenfeld	Bf 109D	39-37
Luftgaukommando III (Berlin)				
Stab JG 2	Oberstlt Gerd von Massow	Döberitz	Bf 109E	3-3
I./JG 2	Maj Carl Vieck	Döberitz	Bf 109E	41-40
10.(N)/JG 2	Hptm Albert Blumensaat	Straussberg	Bf 109D	9-9
Luftgaukommando IV (Dresden)				
Stab JG 3	Oberstlt Max Ibel	Zerbst	Bf 109E	3-3
I./JG 3	Maj Ottheinrich von Houwald	Brandis	Bf 109E	44-38
I./JG 20	Maj Lehmann	Sprottau	Bf 109E	37-36
				335-316

Luftflottenkommando 4 (South-East) HQ: Reihenbach/Silesia

		Base	Type	Est-Serv
Fliegerführer z.b.V (Oppeln)				
JGr.102 (I./ZG 2)	Hptm Hannes Gentzen	Gross-Stein	Bf 109D	45-45
Stab(J)/LG 2	Oberstlt Baier	Nieder-Ellguth	Bf 109E	3-2
Luftgaukommando VIII (Breslau)				
I./JG 76	Hptm Wilfried v Müller-Rienzburg	Ottmütz	Bf 109E	51-45
I./JG 77	Hptm Johannes Janke	Juliusburg-Nord	Bf 109E	48-43
				147-135

istory is nearly 20 minutes late. Most reference sources state that World War 2 began at 05.45 hours on 1 September 1939. This was the time quoted by Adolf Hitler during his address to the *Reichstag* assembly shortly after 10 am on that first morning of hostilities. In the course of his speech, which was broadcast to the German nation, the *Führer* had lambasted the Poles for their 'continuing provocations'. He claimed to be left with no other option than to reply in kind, and therefore 'Fire has now been returned since 05.45 hours'.

To be precise, the opening rounds of 'return' fire – a salvo of 28 cm (11 in) shells from the ex-World War 1 battleship *Schleswig-Holstein* – did not leave their muzzles until 05.47 (04.47 hours local time). They were aimed at point-blank range at the Polish munitions store situated on the tip of the Westerplatte, a sandy promontory just north of the city of Danzig (Gdansk). These shots are regarded by most as the 'official' beginning of World War 2.

But 21 minutes prior to the *Schleswig-Holstein* commencing her bombardment, at 04.26 hours, a *Kette* of Junkers Ju 87 dive-bombers had lifted off from their forward base in East Prussia in what undoubtedly constituted the first overt act of hostility against the Poles. The trio of Stukas of 3./StG 1, led by their *Staffelkapitän* Oberleutnant Bruno Dilley and each carrying one 250 kg bomb plus four smaller 50 kg bombs underwing, immediately set course south-westwards for their target – the iron railway bridge spanning the River Vistula at Dirschau (*Tczew*) – which was just eight minutes flying time away. But their mission was not to destroy the bridge. Despite its size, the Dirschau bridge was the most vulnerable point along the entire 100 km of railway track across the Polish corridor linking the *Reich* proper to its isolated eastern province of East Prussia. It had long been prepared for demolition by the Poles in the event

The first salvoes of World War 2 – the veteran World War 1 battleship *Schleswig-Holstein*, midstream in Danzig's Harbour Canal, has trained its 28 cm (11 in) guns at zero elevation on the Polish positions on the Westerplatte – just 250 metres away – and opened fire!

The first aerial sortie of the war – by Stukas of 3./St.G 1 – failed to prevent demolition of the Dirschau railway bridge (left) by Polish army engineers

of war, and Dilley's objective was the cable which ran along the embankment from nearby Dirschau station out on to the bridge itself. His task was to sever this cable, and thus prevent the Poles from blowing the bridge before the arrival of an armoured train carrying the first German ground troops.

Flying at just ten metres above the mist-shrouded Vistula plain, Dilley and his wingmen scored direct hits on the cable and on the blockhouses protecting the ignition points. But their efforts were to be in vain. The armoured train was held up and the Poles managed to resplice the cable and demolish the bridge at 06.30 hours – just before the German troops could reach it.

While StG 1 can thus lay claim to carrying out the first bombing raid of the war, another *Stukageschwader* – StG 2 'Immelmann' – scored the first aerial kill of the conflict. It was shortly after 04.45 hours that I./StG 2 took off from Nieder-Ellguth in Upper Silesia to attack the Polish airfield at Krakow. On their return the Stukas inadvertently overflew Balice, one of the many secret auxiliary fields to which the bulk of the Polish Air Force had been dispersed during the days leading up to the outbreak of hostilities. Balice housed the PZL P.11s of No 121 Fighter Squadron attached to Army Krakow. Hearing the throb of engines overhead, the squadron commander, Capt Mieczyslaw Medwecki, immediately scrambled with his wingman, Lt Wladek Gnys. At some 300 metres and still climbing, the pair attempted to engage one of the passing Stukas, unaware of another German machine closing in behind them. Leutnant Frank Neubert, flying Ju 87 'Gustav-Kurfürst' (T6+GK), sent a burst of fire from his wing machine-guns into Medwecki's cockpit. The P.11 'suddenly exploded in mid-air, bursting apart like a huge fireball; the fragments literally flew around our ears'. Having just witnessed his luckless squadron commander provide the Luftwaffe with its first aerial victory of the war, Gnys hastily climbed away from the gaggle of Ju 87s only to chance upon a pair of Dornier Do 17E bombers. These were machines of KG 77 likewise returning from the combined early-morning raid on Krakow. Gnys fired at both but then lost sight of them as they disappeared behind a hill. In fact, both Dorniers crashed within 100 metres of each other, littering the village of Zurada with their wreckage. The Luftwaffe's first kill of World War 2 had been quickly followed by its first two losses.

The full-scale commitment of Ju 87 units right fom the start was indicative of the rest of the campaign, for the aerial *Blitzkrieg* against

Aircraft recognition lecture, Polish campaign style. Gym-kitted pilots earnestly study a sand-pit silhouette of what appears to be a twin-tailed biplane – hardly confidence-inspiring for the imminent hostilities!

Frontline flying often meant freedom from the strictures of a peacetime regime, and soon personal aircraft markings began to appear. This unidentified Bf 109E sports one half of the famous cartoon duo *Max und Moritz*, which begs the question was *Moritz* depicted on the other side of that cowling?

Poland was very much the Stuka's war. In conjunction with the longer-range *Kampfgeschwader* and a single *Gruppe* of Henschel Hs 123 ground-assault biplanes, the dive-bombers performed to perfection their assigned task as the army's 'flying artillery', taking out pin-point targets and generally clearing the path for the advancing ground forces. Fighter protection for the Luftwaffe's massive weight of bombers and Stukas was largely in the hands of the new twin-engined Bf 110 *Zerstörer*. The concept of the 'destroyer', or heavy fighter, had yet to reveal its inherent weaknesses, and the Bf 110 was said to be regarded by the Polish Air Force as its most dangerous opponent.

In contrast, the Messerschmitt Bf 109 single-seat fighter played an almost peripheral role in the air war over Poland. The Orders of Battle shown at the start of this chapter for the Luftwaffe's two eastward facing *Luftflotten* indicate that only four Bf 109-equipped *Gruppen* (plus two *Staffeln* of a fifth) were nominally assigned to frontline operational commands, while seven were retained well to the rear under local *Luftgau* (territorial command) control on home defence duties. And of those which *were* engaged over Poland, a number were withdrawn well before the 18-day campaign had run its course. The mere threat of attack from the west following on from the British and French declarations of war on 3 September apparently posed a greater danger in the minds of those in Berlin than did the actual opposition still being offered by the Poles in the east. Indeed, the German capital had already experienced its own version of the famous 'false alarm' which had sent the citizens of London scurrying for their shelters on the first morning of their war, although in Berlin's

Staffel **line-up of JGr.101 (II./ZG 1) at Lichtenau. In the centre, immediately below the 'Running dog' emblem on the Bf 109E and already wearing the Iron Cross, Second Class, is** *Staffelkapitän* **Dietrich Robitzsch (see photo on page 45)**

case the culprit was not an unscheduled airliner coming in from France, but rather a formation of He 111s returning from a raid on Poland!

Nor was the Bf 109's baptism of fire over Poland quite as straightforward and immediately successful as its undoubted superiority as a fighter would lead one to expect.

In the north the units of 1.*Fliegerdivision* were plagued by the same early morning mists which had threatened to jeopardise Bruno Dilley's Stuka attack on the Dirschau bridge. Despite being woken at 03.15, the pilots of Hanns Trübenbach's I.(J)/LG 2 – the fighter component of the Luftwaffe's second *Lehrgeschwader* (Operational Instruction and Evaluation Group) – did not take off until two hours before noon. In all, the *Gruppe* flew four separate escort missions on the opening day of hostilities, but it was 4 September before they first made contact with the Polish Air Force and downed a trio of P.11 fighters. One of the victors was Leutnant Klaus Quaet-Faslem, who would go on to score another 48 kills and rise to become *Gruppenkommandeur* of I./JG 3 before his own death in action against the Americans near Brunswick on 30 January 1944. A number of other pilots who subsequently achieved high-scoring and highly decorated positions of prominence within the *Jagdwaffe* also claimed their first kills during these early days in Poland.

On 9 September I.(J)/LG 2 moved forward to Lauenburg, near Bromberg, in order to keep pace with 4.*Armee* whose advance they were supporting. Here they claimed four more victories – all PWS.26 biplane trainers pressed into emergency reconnaissance and liaison duties – during a *Freie Jagd* sweep of the frontlines. And again, two of the four fell to future aces – Unteroffizier Friedrich Geisshardt and Feldwebel Erwin Clausen, both of whom would be awarded the Oak Leaves and be in command of *Reich's* defence *Gruppen* (III./JG 26 and I./JG 11 respectively) at the time of their deaths in 1943. The following day, 10 September, Geisshardt himself fell victim to P.11 fighters. After several hours in Polish captivity (during which his informal flying garb of Luftwaffe-blue knitted

Unlike the crude emblem decorating the Bf 109 seen on the previous page, the black 'Arched cat' was the official *Staffel* insignia of 2./JG 20 (the later 8./JG 51). The pilot of 'Red 7', here being run up prior to chocks away, was Rudi Rothenfelder, who later transferred to 9./JG 2. In May 1940 he designed that *Staffel*'s famous 'Mosquito' badge, which earned him three days leave!

Back to personal emblems with Josef Heinzeller's 'Black 12', which was named in honour both of his childhood pet dog and his wife! A member of 2.(J)/LG 2, Heinzeller would fly later mark 'Schnauzls' on cross-Channel operations in 1940

sweater had him threatened with a firing squad as a suspected fifth-columnist), he was able to escape during the confusion of a subsequent Stuka raid. He and another captive grabbed a couple of horses and succeeded in reaching friendly territory after a gruelling and dangerous five-day ride.

I.(J)/LG 2 transferred yet further forward on 15 September, this time to Pultusk, some 50 kilometres due north of Warsaw. By now, however, aerial opposition was all but non-existent, and the *Gruppe* was only called on to carry out a few ground-strafing sorties before finally withdrawing to its peacetime base at Garz on 20 September.

Another of 1.*Fliegerdivision's* component units was the naval *Trägergruppe* (Carrier Wing) 186, a mixed formation of one Stuka *Staffel* and two fighter *Staffeln* originally intended for service aboard the as-yet unfinished aircraft carrier *Graf Zeppelin*.

Due to the all-pervading early morning mist, it too was unable to carry out its first scheduled mission of 1 September – aerial cover for the *Schleswig-Holstein* during its bombardment of the Polish enclave on the Westerplatte. But the two Bf 109 *Staffeln* did later escort the Ju 87s of 4.(St)/186 during an attack on the Polish naval base of Hela. According to one pilot, the loss of two of their charges to intense anti-aircraft fire was a salutary introduction to the grim realities of warfare.

The *Staffeln* flew two more Stuka escort missions without incident on 2 September, before transferring to Gutenfeld 24 hours later. Although they remained at this East Prussian base for three days, they saw no further action and returned to Hage on the North Sea coast on 6 September.

Of the two *Jagdgruppen* home-based in East Prussia, I./JG 1 played an even briefer part in the Polish fighting. Major Bernhard Woldenga's precaution of dispersing his *Staffeln* on three separate fields prior to the outbreak of hostilities proved totally unnecessary, as the initial advance of 3.*Armee* southwards out of East Prussia in the direction of Warsaw went all but unopposed by the Polish Air Force. I./JG 1 also flew several ground-strafing missions which resulted in a number of machines suffering damage and one pilot being slightly wounded. But by 4 September (within 24 hours of the Anglo-French declarations of war!) the withdrawal of 1.*Staffel* was already underway and a few days later the entire *Gruppe* was back at its peacetime base at Jesau preparatory to transferring to the western front.

For the other East Prussian *Gruppe*, I./JG 21, the opening day of the Polish campaign was anything but uneventful. From their forward field at Arys-Rostken in the south of the province, they were ordered to escort a formation of He 111s on a raid against Warsaw. Despite the prevailing mist I./JG 21 managed to rendezvous with the bombers, only for the Heinkels' gunners to mistake them for enemy fighters and open fire. The *Gruppenkommandeur,* Hauptmann Martin Mettig, attempted to fire off a recognition signal, but the flare malfunctioned, breaking up and filling the cockpit with a fiery storm of red and white fragments. Wounded in the hand and thigh, and blinded by the smoke, Mettig jettisoned his canopy, losing his aerial mast and antenna in the process. He turned and headed back to base. And the bulk of his *Gruppe*, now out of radio contact with their leader and hampered still by the poor visibility, promptly

followed suit.

It was not until they landed back at Rostken that they learned of the real reason for their early return. Then began an anxious wait for news of those who had carried on. Although the latter had become scattered, it transpired that they had encountered a group of P.11 fighters and had claimed four of the enemy without loss to themselves. One of the victorious pilots was a certain Leutnant Gustav Rödel, yet another future recipient of the Oak Leaves who was to survive the war with 98 victories, all but two of them scored against the western allies.

After their mixed fortunes of the first day, I./JG 21 remained in action against Poland until the end of the campaign, adding two further kills to their scoreboard. The *Gruppe* was finally transferred westwards on 9 October. Meanwhile, to the south, the two *Jagdgruppen* supposedly subordinated to *Luftgau VIII* at Breslau, in Silesia, for homeland defence duties also saw limited action against the Poles.

Hauptmann von Müller-Rienzburg's I./JG 76 was directly descended from the erstwhile Austrian air arm, being created around a cadre drawn from that now defunct service's second *Jagdgeschwader* (*Ja Geschw* II). From its base at Ottmütz, the *Gruppe* deployed to a forward field at Stubendorf upon the outbreak of hostilities. Its first kill – and loss – of the war occurred on 3 September. Some half-dozen Bf 109s of 1./JG 76, led by *Staffelkapitän* Oberleutnant Dieter Hrabak, took off for a *Freie Jagd* sweep of the Tschenstochau (Czestochowa) area. Near Petrikau they spotted a trio of PZL P.23 *Karas* light bombers. Diving to the attack, the German fighters overshot on their first pass – the same thing also happened on their second attack as the Poles attempted to hedge-hop to safety at ground level. In order to reduce their excessive speed the Bf 109 pilots set their propellers to coarse and dumped flap. Wallowing in at about 200 km/h and ignoring the return fire from the *Karas'* rear gunners,

PZL P.23 Karas 'White 9' of No 41 Reconnaissance Squadron, Polish Air Force, reportedly shot down during one of that service's few incursions into German East Prussia

the fighters approached for a third time. One of the Poles was hammered into the ground from a height of 30 metres by a burst from Leutnant Rudolf Ziegler's guns, but fire from the remaining pair hit the *Staffelkapitän*'s radiator. Dieter Hrabak was forced to make an emergency landing behind enemy lines. He successfully evaded, however, and soon rejoined his unit. Despite this inauspicious start, he would rise to become the fifth and final wartime *Kommodore* of JG 54, winning the Oak Leaves and amassing a final total of 125 kills in the process.

I./JG 76 achieved further successes in Poland before departing for the west. One luminary who scored his first kill against the Poles on 5 September went on to even greater heights – Hans 'Fips' Phillip was the fourth pilot to reach a century, and only the second to pass the 200-victory mark. Awarded the Swords to his Oak Leaves, his final score was standing at 206 when, as *Geschwaderkommodore* of JG 1, he was killed in action against P-47s over northern Germany on 8 October 1943 (see *Aircraft of the Aces 9*).

The other Silesian home defence *Gruppe* was I./JG 77. It too opened its score-sheet over Poland with the destruction of three enemy aircraft – all of them P.23 *Karas* reconnaissance-bombers. The first fell to Leutnant Karl-Gottfried Nordmann on 3 September. Nordmann, another later Oak Leaves recipient who ended the war with 78 victories, went one better than his colleagues in I./JG 76 in ensuring his kill. In order to halve his speed to match that of his victim, he did not just extend his flaps – he lowered his undercarriage as well before attacking the *Karas*. Forty-eight hours later the *Gruppe*'s second victory of the Polish campaign went to Hauptmann Hannes Trautloft, one of the enduring figures and outstanding leaders of the *Jagdwaffe* whose final tally of 57 kills included 4 already claimed with the *Condor Legion* in Spain.

Despite the above roll-call of familiar names of those who scored their first kills in Poland, few – if any – achieved more than the one victory described. Their fame was yet to come. The Polish campaign *did* produce one ace, however – a man whose name is now little known despite his score at one time exceeding that of the legendary Werner Mölders; a man whose Iron Cross, First Class, sits modestly alongside the glittering honours later accorded to comrades ten years or more his junior, and a man, moreover, who was a Bf 109 pilot almost by default.

Within the Luftwaffe the concept of the *Zerstörer* went back almost a year, to 1 November 1938, when a distinction was first drawn between 'light' fighters (which were to be controlled by the *Luftgaue* for homeland defence duties) and 'heavy' fighters (to be attached to operational *Fliegerdivisionen* for frontline service). The term 'heavy fighter' was replaced by '*Zerstörer*' on 1 January 1939. The intended equipment for the new *Zerstörergruppen* was to be the equally new twin-engined Bf 110C long-range escort fighter, but problems with the powerplant meant that by the outbreak of the war only three of the ten existing *Zerstörergruppen* had been so equipped. The other seven soldiered on with obsolescent variants of the single-engined Bf 109, five of them having reverted to temporary *Jagdgruppe* designations.

And it was one of these five, *Jagdgruppe* 102 (alias I./ZG 2) based at Gross-Stein, which provided the fighter component of Generalmajor von Richthofen's *Fliegerführer z.b.V.* This was a special-duties command,

Hauptmann Hannes Gentzen, *Gruppenkommandeur* **of JGr.102 (I./ZG 2) and the Polish campaign's sole Bf 109 ace**

otherwise made up of three *Stukagruppen* plus the Luftwaffe's only ground-assault *Gruppe*, which was to form the spearhead of the *Blitzkrieg* offensive aimed at the heart of the Polish defences.

Commanded by 35-year-old Hauptmann Hannes Gentzen, JGr.102 could thus have expected to be in the thick of the action, but even they had a relatively uneventful opening day. A Stuka escort mission to Wielun went unopposed by Polish fighters, the only sign of enemy activity being some light Flak observed at a distance.

The second day of the campaign was to be different. Taking off at first light, Hauptmann Gentzen himself quickly claimed the *Gruppe*'s first kill, bouncing a small formation of Polish bombers and downing one of their number. But honours were to go to Oberleutnant Waldemar von Roon's 1./JGr.102 during a *Freie Jagd* sweep over Lodz later in the morning:

'I was leading the Staffel near Lodz at about 1000 metres and widely echeloned when we spotted two Polish fighters ahead of us, one at a higher altitude. I myself attacked the nearest Pole. My shots must have hit his motor because he immediately started to glide downwards. We followed close on his tail and discovered to our amazement that the spot where he obviously intended to land was a well-camouflaged airfield. We would never have discovered it had we not come down so low, but at this altitude we could clearly make out a row of five enemy bombers, their green-brown camouflage blending perfectly with the earth of the field.

'Meanwhile the aircraft I had damaged nosed over on landing and burst into flames. The pilot jumped out and ran for cover. We flew over

JGr.102's history dates back to its creation as I./JG 232 on 1 April 1936 in Bernburg. In honour of its home town, it adopted the 'Hunter of Bernburg', a much loved local character, as its official badge

One of JGr.102's Bf 109Ds being rearmed ready for its next mission. Note the circular badge just visible below the windscreen

the line of bombers at low level shooting them up. They too went up in flames. Then we spotted a suspicious looking haystack right in the middle of the field. Could it conceal a fuel tanker? Another strafing run. The hay started to burn and revealed four brown-painted fighters hidden underneath. They also caught fire as ground crew ran in all directions like a disturbed ants' nest.

'All this took place on the outskirts of Lodz, right in the middle of some allotments. We must have put on quite an air display for the local citizens!

The bomb-cratered airfield at Krakow provides temporary accommodation for the Bf 109Ds of JGr.102 as they advance eastwards across central southern Poland

'In the meantime the other Pole, who had been circling above us, spiralled down on one of my comrades, who evaded him and banked away. The Pole was then attacked and shot down by the others.'

On the way back to their base at Gross-Stein, von Roon's eight Bf 109Ds encountered four Polish bombers and brought them down too. The *Gruppe's* tally for the day, including Gentzen's earlier victim, stood at 16 – two fighters and five bombers shot down, four fighters and five bombers destroyed on the ground!

JGr.102 continued to fly three or four sorties a day. As aerial opposition dwindled, Hauptmann Gentzen summed up the lot of the Bf 109 pilot in Poland;

'The hardest part is tracking down the enemy fighters. The Pole is a master of concealment, and the olive-brown camouflage of his aircraft is an excellent colour scheme. Once found, bringing them down is quite a bit easier. Although, due to the superior speed of our machines, dogfights occur very seldom. Either you're in a good position and make one pass at high speed – preferably out of the sun – or you go off and hope to find a better target.'

After a few days spent shooting up transport trains and ground strafing columns of troops, JGr.102 moved forward to Krakow. The tented accommodation on this bomb-cratered Polish airfield was a far cry from the luxury they had enjoyed in the chateau back at Gross-Stein, their jumping-off point for the attack on Poland. But the stay at Krakow was to be short-lived and within 48 hours they were on the move again, this time to Debrica. Here they not only had a roof over their heads once more, but also plenty of refreshment with the arrival of a Ju 52 loaded with crates of beer, courtesy of the *Bürgermeister* of their home town, Bernburg!

It was also at Debrica, on 13 September, that a reconnaissance machine was spotted circling overhead, its observer waving to attract attention. A bundle fluttered down – two handkerchiefs tied together containing the message 'Airfield at Brody full of enemy aircraft'. It was signed by the local army commander.

With the promise of a worthwhile target for the first time in days, no time was lost. All available machines were scrambled. Oberleutnant Josef Kellner-Steinmetz's 3./JGr.102, which was already out on patrol, was ordered to follow. Brody (Brodow) was in the far eastern part of Poland, less then 60 kilometres from the Soviet border. The nearby airfield of Hutniki, which was providing temporary refuge for part of the Polish Bomber Brigade, was just a small clearing in the middle of a forest, but Gentzen led his *Gruppe* unerringly to it. As he was about to attack, one of his pilots reported 'Enemy aircraft to port, low'. There, just above the treetops, were eight brown shapes. Gentzen dived on the tails of the unsuspecting Polish two-seaters, who were apparently flying without their rear gunners, and picked off four of them in short order. Others in the *Gruppe* accounted for the rest before attention was turned back to the aircraft on the ground.

Alerted by the noise, the airfield's defenders were ready. One of the Bf 109Ds was hit and disappeared trailing smoke and flames. The remainder inflicted considerable damage, including the reported destruction of several P.37 *Los* bombers, before their fuel situation forced them to break off and head back to Debrica, which was well over 200 km away. Twenty-four hours later they returned to complete the destruction at Brody and to resume the search for the missing Unteroffizier Fritz Linder. In the two days over Brody the *Gruppe* claimed 26 enemy aircraft destroyed in the air and on the ground. Although they found no trace of Linder – an Unteroffizier of the *Reserve* who was the senior physician of a university clinic in private life – the latter had, in fact, successfully crash-landed his burning Messerschmitt and subsequently made his way southwards, despite two fractured vertebrae, into friendly Slovakia.

On 17 September the Soviet Union invaded Poland from the east and the country's fate was sealed. Hauptmann Hannes Gentzen emerged as the campaign's highest scoring Bf 109 pilot, and sole ace, with seven kills to his credit. Altogether, JGr.102 had claimed a total of 78 enemy aircraft destroyed, 29 of them in aerial combat, which made them by far the most successful Bf 109 *Gruppe* in Poland.

Considering the relatively limited number of *Jagdgruppen* actively engaged in the campaign, the Luftwaffe's admitted loss of 67 Bf 109s seems disproportionately high. Many could well have been written off after being damaged by ground fire, but there may have been another contributing factor – I./JG 21's being fired on by the Heinkels they were meant to be escorting on the opening day of hostilities was not an isolated example. 'Friendly fire' incidents on both sides, air-to-air and ground-to-air, were legion throughout the campaign. Polish sources estimate that ten per cent of the Polish Air Force was lost in this way, their own anti-aircraft shooting down twice as many Polish aircraft as was claimed by German Flak. Could the reverse have been true as well? It would certainly explain why Bf 109s suddenly began sporting oversized wing crosses in the months that followed!

The remains of a PZL P.37 Los bomber of the type caught on the ground by JGr.102 at Brody, although the bent propeller blades suggest that this particular example force-landed before burning

GUARDING THE NORTH SEA COAST

Bf 109 Units in North-Western Germany, 1/9/39

Luftflottenkommando 2 HQ: Brunswick

		Base	Type	Est-Serv
Luftgaukommando XI (Hannover)				
II./JG 77	Maj Carl Schumacher	Nordholz	Bf 109E	33-33
Stab ZG 26	Oberst Hans von Döring	Varel	Bf 109D	3-1
I./ZG 26	Hptm Karl Kaschka	Varel	Bf 109D	43-39
JGr.126 (III./ZG 26)	Hptm Johannes Schalk	Neumünster	Bf 109D	46-41
				125-114

The start of the war in the west was a much more clear-cut affair than that in the east had been. Bound by its treaty with the Poles, the British government demanded an undertaking from Hitler that Germany would cease all offensive operations and withdraw its troops from Poland. The deadline was 11 am on the morning of 3 September. No such undertaking was received by that hour and so, in the words and inflection of Prime Minister Neville Chamberlain broadcasting from Downing Street 15 minutes later, '. . . consequently this country *is* at war with Germany'.

Unable materially to help the Poles, Britain and France's (the French had declared war on Germany at 17.30 hours) only option was to adopt an offensive posture in the west, and thereby force Hitler into waging a two-front war. This new western theatre of operations was perforce split into two entirely separate parts – the land front along the Franco-German border, and Germany's open coastline to the north. Between the two lay the Low Countries, whose state of neutrality was at first rigorously observed by both sides – any incursions or overflights were strictly forbidden. It was along Germany's North Sea shores that the first action took place.

At 12.50 hrs., barely 90 minutes after Chamberlain had informed the British people that they were at war, a single Blenheim bomber took off to reconnoitre the German fleet at Wilhelmshaven. The first bombing raids were mounted the following afternoon – a mixed force of 27 Blenheim IVs and Hampdens from five different squadrons were sent to attack warships in the Schillig Roads off Wilhelmshaven, and 14 Wellingtons despatched against the battle-cruisers *Scharnhorst* and *Gneisenau*, which

Ex-*Condor Legion* flyer Feldwebel Alfred Held of 6./JG 77 has been generally credited over the years as being the first Luftwaffe pilot to down an RAF aircraft – a Wellington of No 9 Sqn – in World War 2

The wreckage of two of the four No 107 Sqn Blenheim IVs lost in the first RAF bombing raids of the war – the upturned tail section in the foreground is that of N6184, shot down by naval Flak and recovered from Wilhelmshaven harbour, whilst the fuselage in the background is N6240, which was caught north of Bremerhaven by Leutnant Metz of 4./JG 77 to become the third RAF bomber to fall victim to the Luftwaffe on 4 September 1939

had been located some 80 kilometres to the north-east anchored in the mouth of the River Elbe off Brunsbüttel. Due to the misty conditions, nearly half of the bombers failed to locate their targets, and of the 24 that did, 7 failed to return.

II./JG 77, commanded by Major Carl Schumacher, had arrived at Nordholz – almost equidistant between Wilhelmshaven and Brunsbüttel – only days earlier. Their previous base had been Pilsen, in Bohemia, where they had ostensibly been protecting the nearby Skoda steel-manu-facturing and armaments complex. This *Jagdgruppe* was among the oldest in the Luftwaffe, and could trace its origins back to 1934 when it was first formed as a naval and coastal-protection fighter unit. It had since seen years of service along the North Sea and Baltic coastlines, and somebody in authority must suddenly have awoken to the fact that the *Gruppe*'s unique background and potential was sadly misplaced on a land-locked airfield deep in central Europe.

Schumacher's Bf 109s engaged both enemy formations, but it was two Wellingtons of A Flight, No 9 Sqn, from the Brunsbüttel force which are now recognised as being the first RAF aircraft to fall victim to Luftwaffe fighters in World War 2.

The German pilots involved, both NCOs, recorded their impressions. Feldwebel Alfred Held;

'With the rest of the *Staffel* still quite a way behind me, I already had the Englishman in my sights. I fired my first rounds into the aircraft, but the rear gunner gave as good as he got. Time and again we flashed past each other, machine-guns hammering and engines howling. We had strayed far out over the Jade Bight when the Englishman dived to gain more speed and escape my fire. I forced the Tommy lower and lower and suddenly a long flame shot out from the left side of the bomber. It seemed to be out of control and wallowing about. One final burst was enough. The aircraft dropped its nose and fell. I circled to follow its descent, but already there was just a burning pile of debris in the water which disappeared a few seconds later.'

And Feldwebel Hans Troitzsch;

'We were off the Elbe estuary when I noticed the three Englishmen far below me, very low over the water. When we got nearer I recognised them as twin-engined Wellington bombers. Two immediately made for the low-lying clouds and disappeared. The third was right in front of my guns and I closed in to 100 metres to be certain of hitting him. At 50 metres his port wing broke off and a flame shot from the fuselage. By the time the bomber was engulfed in flames I was only 20 metres behind him. The burning tail broke away and streaked past just above my head. I had to dive to avoid the flames and continued to follow the bomber down. It dropped some 400 metres into the sea where it quickly disappeared, leaving just a slick of oil.'

Both combats were timed simultaneously at 18.15 hours (local time). But it was Held's victory which was officially regarded as the Luftwaffe's 'first' over the RAF, and which was widely proclaimed as such in the contemporary German press. After the war, however, *Gruppenkommandeur* Carl Schumacher went on record as saying he always believed that the honour should have gone to Hans Troitzsch.

Irrespective of who holds rightful pride of place for the first kill, RAF Bomber Command chiefs completely disregarded the fighters' presence. Firm in their belief in the pre-war doctrine that 'the bomber always gets through', they ascribed all their losses to the ferocity and accuracy of the heavy naval Flak over the target areas. The vulnerability of the early Wellingtons' unprotected fuel tanks, even to light machine-gun fire - as witness Held and Troitzsch's both reporting flames shooting from their bombers – was apparently lost on them. September thus witnessed a gradual escalation of two-way traffic across the North Sea as each side sent its bombers to probe at the other's coastal roadsteads and inshore naval anchorages. At this stage it was still very much a gentlemen's war – strictly combatants only – and neither the RAF nor the Luftwaffe was allowed to attack warships actually berthed in harbour for fear of causing civilian casualties.

September also saw II./JG 77 suffer its first two fatalities, both the results of accidents at Nordholz. That on the 17th involved the loss of Feldwebel Alfred Held. The 'Victor of the Jade Bight' of last week's newspaper headlines had earned his place in Luftwaffe history with just one kill.

The next major engagement occurred on 29 September when 11 Hampdens of No 144 Sqn set out on a 'reconnaissance in force' of the

The second contender for Held's title, Feldwebel Hans Troitzsch also of 6./JG 77 claimed the second No 9 Sqn Wellington I brought down off Brunsbüttel at 18.15 hours on 4 September 1939

German Bight. One formation of six aircraft attacked a pair of destroyers without success. The other flight, led by Wg Cdr J C Cunningham, simply failed to return. All five had fallen victim to Luftwaffe fighters, this time the Bf 109Ds of I./ZG 26. Two were claimed by Oberleutnant Günther Specht – on 3 December Specht himself would be shot down off Heligoland by return fire from a Wellington. Forced to ditch in the sea, his facial injuries resulted in the loss of his left eye. Specht nevertheless returned to combat flying, assuming command of II./JG 11 in May 1943. He became one of the outstanding leaders in the defence of the *Reich* and was *Geschwaderkommore* of JG 11 with over 30 victories to his credit, half of them four-engined bombers, when he was killed in the 1945 New Year's Day attack on Allied airfields.

October remained quiet. The apparent lack of enemy activity in the area, combined with that best defence of all – the onset of a North Sea winter – persuaded the Luftwaffe High Command to transfer II./JG 77 back inland. Their destination was Dünstekoven, just outside Bonn. Here they were to form part of the build-up of forces along Germany's *Westwall*.

Hardly had they touched down in the Rhineland, however, before Carl Schumacher was ordered to relinquish command. Promoted to the rank of Oberstleutnant, he was instructed to return forthwith to the German Bight, and there set up a new integrated fighter defence organisation as the '*Jafü Deutsche Bucht*'. Headquartered at Jever, Schumacher spent November gathering his motley forces and establishing radar stations and a communications network covering Germany's North Sea coastline and the outlying islands. The skeleton *Stab* he had inherited, formerly that of the *Jagdgeschwader 'Nord' (ex-JG 77)*, was redesignated to become *Stab Jagdgeschwader 1* on 30 November.

By early December Schumacher was controlling the standard *Geschwader* complement of three *Gruppen*. His old unit, II./JG 77, followed him back from its brief sojourn on the Rhine to deploy two *Staffeln* at Jever and one out on the island of Wangerooge. The *Gruppe* was commanded now by 42-year-old Major Harry von Bülow-Bothkamp, who had led the *Jagdstaffel 'Boelcke'* in World War 1, during which conflict he had been credited with six aerial victories. Since its retirement from Poland, Schumacher's second *Gruppe*, II.(J)/186, had been in north Germany assimilating a new fighter *Staffel* to replace the departed Ju 87s of 4.(St)/186, and slowly re-equipping in its entirety from the Bf 109B on to the newer E-model. It now took up residence at Nordholz under the leadership of Hauptmann Heinrich Seeliger, erstwhile *Staffelkapitän* of 6.(J)/186. Another earlier returnee from Poland, Major Reichardt's JGr.101, comprised Schumacher's third *Gruppe*. Its Bf 109Es made the short hop from Ütersen, dispersing one *Staffel* at Westerland on the island of Sylt and two at Neumünster, north of Hamburg.

In addition to the above, Schumacher also had with him at Jever the remaining parts of ZG 26, which was currently in the process of retraining on Bf 110s and transferring to the western front, and Oberleutnant Johannes Steinhoff's 10.(N)/JG 26. The latter was one of the semi-autonomous nightfighter *Staffeln* hurriedly activated upon the outbreak of war and equipped with obsolescent Bf 109Cs and Ds.

Such then was the strength of the opposition when RAF Bomber

Command decided to resume its offensive across the North Sea. The 3 December raid, during which Günther Specht was wounded, saw 24 Wellingtons return from Heligoland without loss. This only served to reinforce British confidence in the invulnerability of the unescorted daylight bomber when flown in tight formation, and gave rise to a false sense of optimism. But the next raid 11 days later, mounted against the light cruiser *Nürnberg* as it limped for home after taking a torpedo hit from a British submarine, was a very different story.

Alerted by *Freya* radar of the bombers' approach, Schumacher scrambled elements of three units to engage the 12-strong attacking force. It was the Bf 109s of II./JG 77, long wise to the vagaries of the Bight, who, despite the scudding cloud and squalls of sleeting rain, first sighted the dozen Wellingtons of No 99 Sqn and inflicted the most damage. They claimed nine of the attackers destroyed, including two each by Hauptmann Alfred von Loijewski and Feldwebel Erwin Sawallisch, and another by future Knight's Cross fighter and *Zerstörer* ace Unteroffizier Herbert Kutscha, for the loss of one of their own – Leutnant Friedrich Braukmeier. Although the German claims were out by 50 per cent, the five Wellingtons which failed to return, plus a sixth which crashed on landing back at base after suffering damage from a Bf 110 of 2./ZG 26, was a high enough price to pay.

Yet still the RAF hesitated to attribute its losses to enemy fighters. Official investigations into the action were quick to lay the blame elsewhere: the strength and well-directed accuracy of the naval Flak (which had, in fact, scored nil), loss of fuel from punctured wing tanks, even the

The tail of Hans Troitzsch's Bf 109E 'Yellow 5', Wk-Nr 1279, offers a wealth of fascinating detail – three kill markings (the 4 December Wellington, plus two on 18 December), two bullet patches (dated 18/12/39) between and below the arms of the Swastika, the overpainted rectangle of an earlier centre-line Swastika (on a replacement rudder?) and finally the 6.*Staffel* badge depicting a penguin doing something downright rude on Winston Churchill's initials – the latter were a godsend to German 'humorists'!

atrocious weather conditions. Whatever the British view may have been, the Ob.d.L. was in no doubt as to Schumachers success. One result of this latest encounter was the transfer to his command of a twin-engined *Zerstörergruppe* to fill the void left by the departing ZG 26. Hauptmann Reinicke's I./ZG 76 began arriving at Jever from Bönninghardt on 17 December. *Stab* JG 1 now possessed the long-range capability not only to intercept incoming bombers, but also to chase them back out to sea. The Bf 110s could not have come at a more opportune moment.

The morning of Monday 18 December dawned fine and clear. In contrast to the previous week, that day's cloudless, pale-blue wintry sky held the promise of unlimited visibility. The last thing that *Stab* JG 1 therefore expected was a repeat of the costly incursion made by the British four days earlier. This may in part explain the disbelief which greeted the radar sighting reported by the *Freya* station on Wangerooge. For once, Schumacher's elaborate communications system failed him. A combination of misrouted messages and the absence of several *Gruppenkommandeure* away on official business conspired to delay the defenders' response.

The only fighters scrambled in time for any chance of intercepting the raiders during their approach run were six Bf 109Ds of Oberleutnant Steinhoff's 10./(N)/JG 26. Hard on their heels followed the *Alarmrotte* (readiness section) of one of JGr.101's two Neumünster-based *Staffeln*.

Ignoring this initial opposition – if indeed it ever engaged – the 22 Wellingtons which made up the force, still in faultless formation, paraded across Wilhelmshaven at a height of some 4000 metres. But every German naval vessel that drifted into their bombsights was either docked or secure within the confines of the harbour, so no bombs were released.

The first British losses were suffered as the raiders emerged from the coastal Flak barrage, Steinhoff and Feldwebel Willy Szuggar each claiming one Wellington destroyed. It was at this juncture, too, that II./JG 77 and I./ZG 76 joined the fray (alerted too late, II.(J)/186 never made contact with the enemy). For the next 30 minutes a running battle ensued as the bombers, becoming increasingly scattered by the attacks, sought

Oberstleutnant Carl Schumacher, *Jafü* German Bight, in the cockpit of his Bf 109E

individually or in small groups to escape westwards along the Friesian island chain. The longer-legged Bf 110s were the most tenacious of their assailants, the last Wellington of all to succumb finally going down to the guns of Leutnant Uellenbeck of 2./ZG 76 north of the Dutch island of Ameland – over 150 km distant from Wilhelmshaven.

Altogether, Schumacher's pilots claimed the destruction of no fewer than 38 bombers – 15 by I./ZG 76, 14 by II./JG 77 (including two by Feldwebel Hans Troitzsch of 4 September fame, who was himself wounded in the action), six by 10.(N)/JG 26, two by JGr.101 and one by the *Kommodore* himself, who also set off, accompanied by a late starting Bf 109D of Steinhoff's *Staffel*, in pursuit of the bombers;

'I was one of the last to take off. The other *Staffeln* were already under-way. So I climbed into my 109 and gave chase. Visibility was excellent – at 1000 metres you could see a good 50 to 60 kilometres. I set course for the Flak bursts which always gave away the enemy's position. There were columns of smoke hanging in the air from aircraft already shot down – black smoke if they had been hit in the engines, white if the tanks had caught it. A fierce battle was obviously in progress.

'Suddenly I spotted two Englishmen at a height of about 2000 metres. I attacked immediately, but without success. One of the Englishmen dived away, quickly dropping 1000 metres or more, but my 109 was much faster. Too fast, in fact, and so my second pass was unsuccessful as well. I throttled right back, and on this third attempt got on his tail and fired my cannon and machine-guns. Both his engines were hit. It was all over in a second and the Englishman crashed.

'At the same moment I took a burst of well-aimed fire from his wing-man. I immediately banked away, realising my machine had been badly hit. The fuel gauge started to unwind and the stink of benzine filled the cockpit. I tore open the cabin window as I was starting to feel groggy from the fumes. When I properly regained my senses I was only six or seven hundred metres above the sea. With a punctured fuel tank I slowly flew back to base, which I reached with my last drops of fuel. There I experi-enced one of the happiest times of my life. Every machine that returned was waggling its wings. There was hardly one amongst them who did not indicate in this fashion while still in the air that he had scored a kill.'

A subsequent investigation reduced the initial number of claims by about a dozen. Not every pilot was as fortunate as the *Kommodore*, whose success was substantiated by hard evidence – the blackened wreckage of his victim reportedly being visible for days afterwards as it slowly settled

Not Schumacher's victim, but illustrative of the fate of so many early Bomber Command Wellingtons which ended their operational careers in, or under, the shallow waters off the Friesian chain

Bf 109Es of *Stab* II./JG 77 at Jever early in 1940. Note the new light (*hellblau*) fuselage sides and the precautionary use of camouflage matting to hide the large-size fuselage crosses. In the foreground is the machine of *Gruppenkommandeur* Major Harry von Bülow-Bothkamp

in the shallow *Watt*, or tidal mud-flats, off the island of Spiekeroog.

But even 26 British bombers downed for the loss of just two pilots killed and several others wounded was a major victory. The 'Battle of the German Bight' was trumpeted by the German press and in the newsreels (partly, it has been suggested by some, to soften the blow to national pride suffered by the scuttling of the pocket battleship *Graf Spee* in the mouth of the River Plate the day before). At one of the many receptions held afterwards, Schumacher was even able to make capital of the breakdown in communications which had denied II.(J)/186 a part in the battle. Summoned to Berlin by Goering, the *Kommodore* and six of his most successful pilots attended a press conference. Here Schumacher, tongue no doubt firmly in cheek, was able to assure the assembled reporters, both German and neutral, that so confident had he been of his units' ability to handle anything the RAF could throw at them, he had not felt it necessary to commit his entire strength but had, in fact, 'kept whole *Staffeln* in reserve'!

There was no such levity on the other side of the North Sea when the actual cost of the battle was counted. Of the 22 Wellingtons which had reached and crossed Wilhelmshaven, 11 had been shot down while running the gauntlet of attacks from Wangerooge to Ameland, and another had later ditched in the sea. Six more crashed, or crash-landed, with varying degrees of damage after reaching the English coast.

But the real measure of the 'Battle of the German Bight' was felt not in terms of immediate losses and successes, but rather in the effect it had on each side. For the British the message of the unescorted daylight bomber had finally been driven home. For the remainder of the war Bomber Command would carry the fight to the shores of Germany and beyond almost exclusively under the cover of darkness.

For Schumacher, his very success, and the subsequent relative dearth of RAF activity in his area by day, had rendered him virtually redundant. Over the course of the next five months only some dozen recce bombers would be claimed by his subordinate units. The first of these, an incautious Blenheim, fell to the *Kommodore* off Wangerooge on 27 December. It was mid-February 1940 before Unteroffizier Kutscha of II./JG 77 claimed a second. On 27 February Oberleutnant Jahnny downed yet another to finally provide II.(J)/186 with its first kill of the war.

Another two months were to pass before the destruction of a mine-laying Hampden off Sylt on the night of 25/26 April by Oberfeldwebel Hermann Förster of IV.(N)/JG 2 marked the opening of a new chapter in Luftwaffe history. This *Gruppe* had been formed on 15 February by the amalgamation of the three hitherto separate single-engined nightfighter units, 10.(N)/JG 2, 10.(N)/JG 26 and 11.(NJ)/LG 2, and Förster's Hampden is believed to be the first Bomber Command aircraft to be intercepted and shot down by a Luftwaffe nightfighter.

Exactly two weeks later Schumacher's pilots were to forsake – at least temporarily – their by now almost routine guardianship of Germany's North Sea coastline. The invasion of Holland was about to begin.

PATROLLING THE WESTWALL

Bf 109 Units in Central and South-Western Germany, 1/9/39

Luftflottenkommando 2 HQ: Brunswick

		Base	Type	Est-Serv
Luftgaukommando VI (Münster)				
Stab JG 26	Oberst Eduard Ritter von Schleich	Odendorf	Bf 109E	3-2
I./JG 26	Maj Gotthardt Handrick	Odendorf	Bf 109E	44-43
II./JG 26	Hptm Herwig Knüppel	Bönninghardt	Bf 109E	38-38
I./JG 52	Hptm Dietrich Graf von Pfeil und Ellguth	Bonn-Hangelar	Bf 109E	48-38
II./ZG 26	Maj Friedrich Vollbracht	Werl	Bf 109D	48-45
11.(N)/LG 2	Oblt Bascilla	Cologne-Ostheim	Bf 109D	9-9
				190-175

Luftflottenkommando 3 HQ: Roth, near Nuremberg

		Base	Type	Est-Serv
5. Fliegerdivision (Gersthofen near Augsburg)				
JGr.152 (I./ZG 52)	Hptm Lessmann	Biblis	Bf 109D	48-45
6. Fliegerdivision (Frankfurt-on-Main)				
JGr.176 (II./ZG 76)	Hptm Schmidt-Coste	Gablingen	Bf 109D	50-42
Luftgaukommando VII (Munich)				
I./JG 51	Hptm Ernst Freiherr von Berg	Eutingen	Bf 109E	46-32
I./JG 71	Maj Kramer	Fürstenfeldbruck	Bf 109D	34-34
Luftgaukommando XII (Wiesbaden)				
Stab JG 53	Oberst Hans Klein	Wiesbaden-Erbenheim	Bf 109E	3-3
I./JG 53	Hptm Lothar von Janson	Kirchberg	Bf 109E	46-38
II./JG 53	Hptm Günther von Maltzahn	Mannheim-Sandhofen	Bf 109E	44-38
Luftgaukommando XIII (Nuremberg)				
I./JG 70	Maj Kithil	Herzogenaurach	Bf 109D	50-21
				321-253

lthough the Franco-German border regions witnessed no major air action to equal the 'Battle of the German Bight', the level of aerial activity along the western front hardly merited the term 'Phoney War'. True, the opposing ground forces, each side safely ensconced behind its own line of defence ('Maginot' and 'Siegfried' – ie *Westwall* – respectively), initially displayed little desire to disturb the status quo. But such inertia was not mirrored in the skies above. The opening eight months of the air war in the west were marked by an escalating series of small-scale, but nonetheless bitterly fought, engagements – the intervening winter months permitting – as both sides' fighters sought to defend their airspace against hostile incursions, first by individual reconnaissance aircraft and later by flights of bombers.

And unlike the relatively limited and stable number of *Jagdgruppen* deployed in the northern coastal provinces, the fighter units gathering along the *Westwall* received a steady influx of reinforcements. These were provided not only by the lion's share of the exodus from Poland, and by the transfer forward of units from the hinterland *Luftgaue* once Berlin's earlier fears of an Anglo-French strategic bombing offensive had receded, but also by the activation of new *Jagdgruppen* intended to bring to full establishment those *Geschwader* which had begun the war only one or two *Gruppen* strong.

It was one of these latter brand new *Jagdgruppen* which was to achieve the Luftwaffe's first kill on the western front. Such was the unpreparedness of the British and French for war that nothing actually happened for the first few days. During that time, however, II./JG 52 had been formed (out of 11./JG 72) at Böblingen under Hauptmann Hans-Günther von Kornatzki, who was to become famous as the originator of the Fw 190 *Sturm* tactics later employed to such telling effect in defence of the *Reich* (see *Aircraft of the Aces 9*).

On 8 September a *Rotte* (two-aircraft section) of Bf 109Ds from II./JG 52 was patrolling the Rhine when it spotted a French reconnaissance aircraft taking an interest in the bridge at Kehl. The fighters chased it off and, after one unsuccessful pass, a second attack from astern by Leutnant Paul Gutbrod caused the luckless Mureaux 115 to break up in the air. Gutbrod received the Iron Cross, Second Class, for this exploit, but was himself killed on 1 June 1940 during a ground-attack on French troops near Belval in the Ardennes.

Earlier that same day the first reported clash between fighters of the Luftwaffe and the Armée de l'Air had taken place in the adjoining sector, just to the north of Karlsruhe, when a *Schwarm* (four-aircraft flight) of Bf 109Es from I./JG 53 had 'bounced' six French Curtiss H-75A Hawks. Although the outcome was inconclusive, the *Schwarmführer's* machine had been hit in the engine. Attempting a forced landing in a field near Wölfersweiler, the pilot suffered slight injuries when the Bf 109's undercarriage sank into the soft ground at 120 km/h and the aircraft somersaulted over on to its

A *Schwarm* of Bf 109Es. This tactical grouping of four fighters, perfected in Spain by Werner Mölders, gave the *Jagdwaffe* a decisive advantage over the RAF's more rigid vic and line-astern formations in the early engagements over France and the Low Countries

back. Despite the combined efforts of three hefty farm labourers to try to lift the wreckage, Oberleutnant Werner Mölders, the top-scoring fighter pilot of the *Condor Legion* in Spain with 14 victories already to his credit, remained trapped in the cockpit. He was finally released by troops from a nearby Flak unit, but had to spend the next few days laid up with a strained back. The *Staffelkapitän* of 1./JG 53 thus missed the next morning's engagement which saw one of his own *Staffel* pilots, Oberfeldwebel Walter Grimmling, open JG 53's score with the destruction of a Bloch 131 reconnaissance-bomber. A second Bloch 131 was claimed by JG 52. That afternoon two more – Bloch 200s this time – provided JGr.152 with their first kills of the war.

In the weeks and months that followed a whole succession of such 'firsts' would be achieved, or suffered, by the *Jagdgruppen* along the *Westwall* – be they only recently activated or units of five years' standing or more – as each experienced its baptism of fire against the French or British, claimed its opening victories and sustained its initial losses. The 'Phoney War' period also witnessed the emergence of dozens of fledgling aces – pilots whose names would later become familiar both at home and abroad, as they achieved the first of what were to grow into long lists of kills, many topping the 100 mark, and one even surpassing 200.

But the next pilot to open his score against the French (having already returned with four victories from Spain) has since become well known for quite a different reason. Oberleutnant Rolf Pingel, *Staffelkapitän* of 2./JG 53, would add 21 more kills to the Mureaux reconnaissance machine he destroyed on 10 September before – as *Gruppenkommandeur* of I./JG 26 – he was himself brought down near Dover on 10 July 1941, his forced landing presenting the RAF with an almost undamaged specimen of the Luftwaffe's then latest fighter, the Bf 109F-1.

20 September heralded the beginning of the rise to even greater fame of the *Condor Legion*'s highest scorer. Recovered from his back injury, Werner Mölders claimed his first kill of World War 2 by despatching one of the two French Hawk H-75As lost on that date. The first RAF casualties were also suffered on the same day – two Fairey Battles of No 88 Sqn going down under the guns of the Bf 109Ds of JGr.152. Four days later another JGr.152 pilot and future ace, Leutnant Hartmann Grasser, destroyed a Hawk to begin his climb to a grand total of 103 victories.

But it was on 25 September that the most successful of all fighter pilots to cut his teeth against the French first made his mark when Feldwebel Heinz Bär of 1./JG 51, who would end the war as an Oberstleutnant flying Me 262 jets and with 220 victories to his credit, shot down yet another of the seemingly ubiquitous French Hawks.

The last day of the month was marked by some of the fiercest clashes yet to have taken place, and again it was I. and II./JG 53 who were involved. By the day's end the

This line-up of future JG 53 aces would together account for a final tally of over 600 enemy aircraft destroyed. Left to right; Ernst Klager (22), Kurt Brändle (180), Wolf-Dietrich Wilcke (162), Günther von Maltzahn (68), Heinz Bretnütz (35), Stefan Litjens (38), Hans-Heinrich Brustellin (4), Erich Schmidt (47) and Franz Götz (63)

'Ace-of-Spades' pilots had claimed no less than 13 kills – including an entire formation of five Fairey Battles from No 150 Sqn – for the loss of four of their own number. Among the victors were Hauptmann Günther von Maltzahn, *Kommandeur* of II.*Gruppe*, Wolfgang Lippert and Josef Wurmheller, all future highly-decorated *Experten*.

The Bf 109E of Oberst Gerd von Massow, *Geschwaderkommodore* of JG 2, pictured at Frankfurt-Rebstock in early 1940. Note the *Geschwader* badge and standard *Kommodore* chevron and bars markings, plus the additional '1' (presumably to indicate von Massow's position in the *Stabsschwarm*) and the small size of the fuselage cross compared to von Bülow-Bothkamp's machine seen on page 25

Although the front was relatively quiet during October, both sides utilised the lull to build up their strength. Yet more new *Jagdgruppen* were brought into being, and several existing units were redeployed forward to bolster the most hotly contested stretch of airspace – that running south-eastwards from the lower tip of Luxembourg, along the Saarland and Palatinate borders, to Karlsruhe.

This sector was particularly active because it formed the northernmost part of the common Franco-German frontier, which diverged when it reached the Duchy of Luxemburg at the so-called *Dreiländereck* (literally three nations corner). From there northwards to the sea the two warring sides were separated by the neutral Low Countries. The region immediately south of the *Dreiländereck* thus offered the shortest route of entry for Allied reconnaissance aircraft seeking to turn the neutrals' flank and probe the secrets of what lay behind them, including Germany's industrial heartland of the Ruhr. But so successful was JG 53 in defending this sensitive area that most such sorties were nipped in the bud. Few Allied aircraft managed to penetrate their sector and then turn northwards, which may explain in part why *Luftflotte* 2's *Jagdgruppen* (including those of JG 26 and the later JGs 27, 51 and 54) deployed above Cologne in the lee of neutral Holland saw such little activity in the months prior to May 1940.

One *Staffel* of Hauptman von Kornatzki's II./JG 52 was particularly pleased to be moving nearer to the front. It had proved so quiet back in Böblingen, apart from the occasional nocturnal intruder, that higher command had decreed that one of von Kornatzki's *Staffeln* should give up its Bf 109s and convert on to Heinkel He 51 biplanes for ad hoc night-fighter duties. Confusingly, two of the *Gruppe*'s *Staffelkapitäne* bore the same name – Oberleutnant Heinz Schumann commanded 4./JG 52, while Oberleutnant August Wilhelm Schumann (who also answered to the names Sven or 'Rabatz') headed 5./JG 52. To simplify matters they were known respectively as 'Long' and 'Short' Schumann, and it was the latter who was to re-equip. So vehemently did he protest, however, that he was finally allowed to keep his Bf 109s – but a dozen He 51s nonetheless arrived a few days later. So, for several weeks, 5./JG 52 found themselves in the curious – not to say unique – position of operating the Messerschmitts by day and the Heinkels by night! It was not until the whole *Gruppe* transferred forward to Lachen-Speyerdorf that the scheme was abandoned and the elderly biplanes happily left behind.

One of October's new *Gruppen* was III./JG 53, command of which

Judging from the oxygen mask, this pilot (believed to be of 2./JG 27) is preparing for a high-altitude patrol of the Dutch border

was entrusted to Hauptmann Werner Mölders. And just as in September, so this second month of the air war in the west also ended in a sudden flurry of action. On the afternoon of 30 October three Blenheim Is of No 18 Sqn took off from Metz to reconnoitre areas of north-western Germany. One never made it. It fell foul of more than a dozen patrolling Bf 109s of III./JG 53 near Trier, providing the *Gruppe* with its first kill of the war, and Werner Mölders with his second. Another got as far as Osnabrück before it was finally intercepted by a *Rotte* of Bf 109s of I./JG 21. Since its return from Poland exactly three weeks earlier, this *Gruppe* had converted from the Bf 109D to the newer E-model. And it was the *Emil* flown by future ace and Knight's Cross recipient, Leutnant Heinz Lange, which claimed the Blenheim – Lange, coincidentally, would end the war as *Kommodore* of JG 51, the *Geschwader* which was to bear Mölder's name.

On 6 November Leutnant Max Stotz of I./JG 76 – yet another earlier participant in the Polish campaign and subsequent highly-decorated ace with 189 kills to his credit before his loss in Russia in August 1943 – scored his first by shooting down a No 57 Sqn Blenheim I near Frankfurt. But that day also saw the largest engagement of the air war over the western front to date – and the *Jagdwaffe*'s costliest reversal. Major Hannes Gentzen had taken off from Lachen-Speyerdorf at the head of 27 Bf 109Ds of his JGr.102 to patrol the River Saar, only to meet nine French Hawk H-75As of GC II/5 escorting a Potez 63 reconnaissance machine over the same area. An attempted 'bounce' quickly degenerated into a series of individual skirmishes which lost Gentzen four pilots, including two of his *Staffelkapitäne,* Oberleutnante von Roon und Kellner-Steinmetz. Four more machines force-landed with major damage and one pilot wounded. The *Gruppe's* sole success was one of the H-75As credited to the *Kommandeur.* But this was insufficient to prevent Gentzen's immediately being summoned to Berlin to report on the debacle in which JGr.102 had suffered over 25 per cent casualties to a force one-third of its size. The main conclusion seemed to be that its Bf 109Ds, which had swept all before them in Poland, were no match for aggressively flown Hawks. The *Gruppe* was transferred to a quieter sector a few days later, and subsequently began its long-awaited conversion onto the Bf 110. Gentzen's ninth victory was to be achieved on the twin-engined *Zerstörer* when he downed another H-75A over the Argonne on 7 April 1940. At this stage he was still just one ahead of Werner Mölders in the scoring stakes, but would add no more before his death in an emergency scramble the following month. It was on 26 May 1940, at the height of the campaign in France, that RAF Battles launched a surprise raid on the now I./ZG 2's base of Neufchateau. Gentzen had dashed for his Bf 110, calling for the *Gruppen-Adjutant* to take the rear-gunner's seat. But while still clawing for height the aircraft's tail caught the tops of the trees bordering the field and it crashed. Neither occupant had had time to strap himself in, and both were killed instantly.

Twenty-four hours after JGr.102's drubbing of 6 November, two more very familiar names were to make their mark with the first of a long succession of kills each – Leutnant Joachim Müncheberg of III./JG 26 shooting another Blenheim I of No 57 Sqn into the Rhine north of Cologne, and Hauptmann Wolf-Dietrich Wilcke, one of Mölders' *Staffelkapitäne* in III./JG 53, despatching a reconnaissance Potez 637 over the Saar. Having opened their scores on the same day, their subsequent progress would continue to display marked similarities. Both had received the Swords to their Oak Leaves and had risen to the command of *Geschwader* with well over 100 victories apiece (Müncheberg of JG 77 with 135, Wilcke of JG 3 with 162) before their deaths in action against Allied fighters exactly one year apart to the day – the former versus Spitfires in North Africa on 23 March 1943, and the latter against Mustangs over the *Reich* on 23 March 1944.

On 22 November another pair of future aces and Oak Leaves recipients claimed their first victims. One, Oberleutnant Hermann-Friedrich Joppien of I./JG 51, downed a Morane-Saulnier MS.406 and survived a crash-landing after the engagement to go on to achieve 69 further victories before being killed in Russia in August 1941. The other was a member of I./JG 2, the *Gruppe* which had been fruitlessly guarding Berlin since the beginning of the war but which had now finally been moved forward to the western front, where it had arrived at Frankfurt-Rebstock exactly one week earlier.

The combat career of 24-year old Leutnant Helmut Wick, which began with the destruction of a Hawk H-75A of GC II/4 on this day, was little short of meteoric. His rise from relative obscurity as a *Rottenführer* (section leader) in 3.*Staffel* to *Geschwaderkommodore* of JG 2 'Richthofen' within the space of a year remains unparalleled in the annals of the Luftwaffe. Wick described his first kill for the Luftwaffe magazine *Der Adler*. It typifies the free-wheeling fighter duels which were taking place above the static fortifications of the western front in those early months of war;

'As the French did not cross the German border very often, my wingman and I decided for once to visit them. A tailwind from the east helped us on our way. Near Nancy I suddenly saw a gaggle of aircraft at an altitude of some 6000 metres. Realising immediately that they were not German, we began to circle. Two aircraft detached themselves from the bunch above and swooped down on us. Now I could recognise them – Curtiss fighters.

'We dived away and, just as we had anticipated, the two Frenchmen dived after us. I went into a climbing turn with one of the Frenchmen right on my tail. I can still clearly remember how I could

Arguably the greatest of them all, Hauptmann Werner Mölders describes a recent encounter with a Blenheim I of No 18 Sqn on 30 October 1940; 'I took off with the *Gruppenschwarm* and three *Schwärme* of 9.*Staffel* to patrol against enemy reconnaissance aircraft in the Bitburg-Merzig area. At 11.12 I noticed Flak activity near Trier. I approached to within 50 metres of the enemy aircraft without being seen, and saw the British roundel very clearly. I opened fire and closed to the shortest possible range without any return fire from the rear gunner, and the left engine gave out a thick white cloud of smoke. It changed very quickly to black. When I pulled up beside it, the aircraft burned completely. I observed a parachute, but it seemed to kindle'. This unrecognisable pile of debris in the woods above Trier was all that remained of Mölders' Blenheim I (L6694, flown by Flt Lt A A Dilnot), which was caught by the *Jagdflieger* (at centre of the trio on the right) while attempting to negotiate the 'Dreiländereck'

see his red, white and blue roundels when I looked behind me. At first, the sight of them was rather exciting, particularly as the Frenchman was firing away with everything he had. But then the realisation that somebody is behind you and shooting at you is very unpleasant.

'I pushed the nose down again and, with my superior speed, quickly lost him. When my Frenchman was no longer to be seen, I

Having finally converted on to the Bf 110C and assumed its rightful identity as I./ZG 2 (note the 'Hunter of Bernburg' badge below the cockpit), it was in a machine such as this that Hauptmann Hannes Gentzen was to lose his life on 26 May 1940

looked up to my left to find the others. Not a thing in sight. I glanced up to my right and could hardly believe my eyes. I was staring straight at four radial engines all sprouting little red flames. A ridiculous thought flashed through my mind – "Are they really allowed to shoot at me like that?"

'But then I was all concentration. Should I try to get away again? No! Now's the time to tackle them. One has *got* to go down. Clenching my teeth, I hauled the stick and rudder to the right and turned into them.

'By the time I had completed my turn the first had already shot past me. The second was right behind him, and this one I attacked head-on. It was a nasty moment looking straight down his blazing gun barrels, but we were too close to score any hits. He zoomed over my head and now the third one was almost on top of me.

'I manoeuvred my aircraft slightly to get him nicely lined up in my sights, aiming and firing just as I had been taught at fighter training school. With my first shots I saw some pieces of metal fly off the Frenchman. Then both his wings buckled and gave way.

'Close behind him the fourth Curtiss was also firing at me, but I was not hit. The first pair were now climbing again. I followed suit so that they could not catch me. I was getting low on fuel and it was time to head for home. My wingman, who had returned to base safe and sound, had lost me after the first dive in all the twisting and turning.'

Wick concluded his account by confessing that the action had very nearly not taken place at all. Just before take-off his aircraft had been washed down and while climbing to altitude on the outward flight ice had begun to form. He had been in two minds whether to return to base. These freezing conditions, which were to blanket the whole of the western front in thick snow, heralded the start of one of the region's worst

On 22 November 1939 – the day which saw both Wick and Joppien score their firsts – two Bf 109Es landed intact behind French lines. This is 'White 14' (Wk-Nr 1304) of 1./JG 76 which was test flown by the French, as shown here, before being handed over to the British for evaluation at Farnborough as AE479. Later still this much-travelled *Emil* was shipped to the USA

winters for decades. Flying was to be severely restricted for the best part of three months.

It was during this period, however, that the first clash between Luftwaffe and RAF fighters finally occurred. On 22 December it was Mölder's III./JG 53 – who else – who were escorting a pair of Do 17 reconnaissance aircraft along the Saar when they spotted three enemy fighters far below them. Diving to

Long overshadowed by the ebullient Hans 'Assi' Hahn of JG 2 (see *Aircraft of the Aces 9*), Hans 'Vadder' von Hahn used the same play on words as his namesake to devise a personal emblem, '*Hahn*' meaning 'Cockerel' in German. This is an early version sported during his service as *Gruppen-Adjutant* of II./JG 53

Early in 1940 II./JG 51, based at Friedrichshafen on the shores of Lake Constance, was the southernmost of all the *Jagdgruppen* gathered along the *Westwall*. Feldwebel Johann Illner's 'White 9' takes some of the sting out of the *Gruppe's* rather belligerent 'Gott strafe England' badge by adding the names *Hänschen* and *Gretl* behind it!

the attack, Mölders picked off the machine to the left in a single pass, whilst that on the right fell moments later to the *Staffelkapitän* of 8./JG 53, Oberleutnant Hans von Hahn (another future ace and Knight's Cross holder). Both fighters, initially identified as MS.406s, went down trailing smoke and flames, Mölder's victim obviously out of control and von Hahn's went straight in 'like a fiery comet'. In fact, they were Hurricane Is of No 73 Sqn's A Flight, their sergeant-pilots (J Winn and R Perry), it later transpired, both being killed instantly by the opening rounds of machine-gun fire.

Although the weather continued to deteriorate into the opening weeks of the new year, 10 January 1940 offered a rare opportunity for a pilot of one of the southernmost *Jagdgruppen* along the Upper Rhine sector to begin his rise to 100+ acedom. Oberleutnant Reinhard Seiler had already claimed nine victories with the *Condor Legion* in Spain, and was a member of I./JG 70 upon the outbreak of war. When that *Gruppe* was redesignated I./JG 54 and moved forward to Eutingen, he became *Kapitän* of 1.*Staffel*. It was while leading a *Schwarm* of 1./JG 54 that he scored his first kill – a low-flying Potez 63 returning from a reconnaissance of the Freiburg area, which he shot down less than ten kilometres from the Swiss border north-east of Basle.

By the end of the third week in March conditions had improved sufficiently to allow a resumption of activity. One of the earliest RAF losses of this final stage of the 'Phoney War' was UK-based Photographic Development Unit (PDU) recce Spitfire N3069 – the first of its kind to be brought down – which was caught by Bf 109Es of I./JG 20 on 22 March hard by the Dutch border south of Arnhem.

Four days later a further clash between those old adversaries, III./JG 53 and No 73 Sqn, was to result in material damage to both sides. After a scrappy series of engagements over the Saar, three of the Bf 109s force-landed back at Trier, while Kiwi Flg Off E J 'Cobber' Kain (later to become the RAF's first ace) had to take to his parachute when his Hurricane was shot out from under him by Feldwebel Weigelt. Hauptmann Mölders also claimed another 'MS.406' for his sixth victory. Whatever the undoubted qualities of the immortal Mölders as a fighter pilot, aircraft recognition did not come high on the list! His supposed

victim was, in fact, the Hurricane flown by Flg Off N 'Fanny' Orton (also later to make ace) which, although damaged, managed to regain its base.

On the last day of March MS.406s did provide the opposition – or, more accurately, the targets – when a formation of the French fighters was caught completely unawares by II./JG 53, who claimed six of their number in a matter of moments. One was the second victory for *Gruppenkommandeur* 'Henri' Maltzahn. Three of the others also fell to future well-known aces – one to Leutnant Gerhard Michalski and a brace to Oberleutnant Heinz Bretnütz, although the latter's claiming of a Wellington some four hours later would seem to be another example of misidentification.

Mölders got another Hurricane on 2 April, this time forcing Plt Off C D 'Pussy' Palmer of No 1 Sqn to 'take to the silk'. It was 18 days before he claimed his next, a Hawk H-75A east of Saarbrücken. 20 April saw two other highly successful ex-*Condor Legion* pilots achieve kills – Oberleutnant Otto 'Otsch' Bertram (8 Spanish victories) of I./JG 2 also downing a Hawk H-75A near Saarbrücken, and Hauptmann Horst 'Jakob' Tietzen, *Staffelkapitän* of 5./JG 51 (7 victories in Spain), catching a French reconnaissance Bloch 174 south-west of Strasbourg. That evening, too, a Fairey Battle of No 218 Sqn out dropping leaflets over Darmstadt and Mainz fell victim to a Bf 109D flown by Oberfeldwebel Willi Schmale of IV.(N)/JG 2. This is believed to be not only the last Battle lost in action during the 'Phoney War', but also the first Luftwaffe nightfighter kill of the war, preceding Förster's destruction of a Hampden off Sylt by five days, and the first 'official' victory of the established nightfighter arm by nearly three months – the latter was also credited to Förster whilst still flying the Bf 109, but now as a member of III./NJG 1, when he downed a Whitley off Heligoland in the early hours of 9 July 1940.

Twenty-four hours later another high-flying PDU Spitfire (N3071) was intercepted south of Stuttgart by half-a-dozen Bf 109Es of II./JG 51, which had appproached unseen from astern under cover of their quarry's contrail. With his engine damaged by cannon fire, the PR pilot baled out to become a PoW. Although two future aces – Oberleutnant Josef 'Joschko' Fözö and Leutnant Erich Hohagen (with final scores of 27 and 55 respectively) – were numbered among the six pursuers, the destruction of the Spitfire was credited to Oberfeldwebel Johann Illner, who himself later became a PoW after baling out over Essex on 5 November with a more modest final tally of 7.

On 23 April Hauptmann Mölders claimed his ninth, and final, victory of the 'Phoney War' – Sgt C N S Campbell, who was one of two No 73 Sqn pilots downed by III./JG 53 on that day. Thereafter fighter activity declined as the Luftwaffe began to prepare itself for the forthcoming attack on France and the Low Countries.

That the air war along the western front during 1939-40 had been anything but 'phoney' is best illustrated by the fact that the *Jagdgruppen* had claimed some 160 kills during the period, 73 alone going to JG 53, the *Geschwader* responsible throughout for protecting the vital Saar sector. And if the campaign in Poland had produced its Gentzen, and the defence of the northern seaboard its Schumacher, then one name above all others emerges from the ranks of the aerial duellists along the *Westwall* – Werner Mölders.

Mid-March 1940 and still no let up in the wintry weather, as witness this well wrapped-up trio 'somewhere on the Western front'

Future *Experten* Leutnant Erich Hohagen (centre) and Oberleuntnant Josef Fözö (right) appear to sympathise with a somewhat dejected looking Flg Off Cecil Milne, pilot of Spitfire PR IA N3071 shot down by the now Oberfeldwebel Illner (he of the 'Hänschen und Gretl' markings on page 33) on 21 April 1940. The British pilot later recounted, 'Six Messerschmitts approached under my "contrail" but I did not see them as I was busy photographing. The leader put a cannon shell into my engine which rapidly failed. While it lasted I tried to get back to France, suffering further attacks on the way. Thirty miles from the frontier, at a few thousand feet, the engine gave out so I baled out between attacks, after putting the Spitfire into a dive to destroy its equipment. I landed in a village and was immediately arrested'

SCANDINAVIAN SIDESHOW

Bf 109 Unit in the Norwegian Campaign, 9/4/40

X Fliegerkorps HQ: Hamburg

		Base	Type	Est-Serv
II./JG 77	Hptm Karl Hentschel	Husum	Bf 109E	37-29

Before unleashing his forces against France and the Low Countries, Hitler had despatched part of the Wehrmacht northwards on one of its earliest strategic forays. The invasion of Norway on 9 April 1940 was all about safeguarding Germany's supply of Swedish iron ore, which was shipped via the Norwegian port of Narvik, and the equally determined – though woefully less well-prepared and equipped – Anglo-French expedition to cut off that supply.

Because of the distances involved, the twin-engined *Zerstörer* units played the dominant fighter role in the opening phases. It was they who escorted the Ju 52 transports carrying the airborne invasion troops. The Bf 109s of II./JG 77, released from their long months of patrolling the German Bight and commanded now by Hauptmann Karl Hentschel, followed up in stages – from Husum to Aalborg and Esbjerg in Denmark, and thence the short hop across the Skagerrak on 11 April to Kristiansand-Kjevik, a small civil airfield in southern Norway which was the first stop on DNL airlines' coastal-hugging route from the capital Oslo up to Tromsö above the Arctic Circle.

Once arrived, however, Hentschel's pilots found Norwegian waters much more alive with enemy air activity than the German seaboard had been of late. Within 24 hours elements of 5. and 6./JG 77 were scrambled to engage an incoming formation of RAF bombers – 12 Hampdens of Nos 44 and 50 Sqns intent on attacking German naval vessels in Kristiansand harbour. In a running 15-minute battle the Bf 109s claimed exactly half of the Hampdens, two falling to the guns of Feldwebel Robert Menge. But the encounter was far from one-sided. Return fire from the bombers downed five of their assailants, with four pilots being killed and the fifth wounded. Ten minutes later a separate *Rotte* on routine patrol destroyed a Coastal Command Hudson of No 233 Sqn in the same area south-west of Kristiansand.

II./JG 77 was now responsible for providing the aerial defence of Norway's southern and western coastline. In order to do so, the individual *Staffeln* were split up and deployed on the few existing fields in the area.

35

There was little ground organisation, and each was left very much to its own devices. But the greatest drawback was the almost complete lack of any form of early-warning system. Unlike the German Bight, with its chain of *Freya* radar stations, the Norwegian coast was an open door. The *Staffeln* had to fly standing patrols, relying on a virtually blind ground-control whose directions were often inaccurate and invariably late. On one classic occasion a *Rotte* of Bf 109s at Stavanger were given the emergency scramble order and instructed to climb to 4000 metres, only for RAF bombers to slip in below them and attack the field from a height of 200 metres.

These two shots of II./JG 77 *Emils* illustrate the change in camouflage finish during the *Gruppe's* service in Norway, the standard *hellblau* scheme of early 1940 as still worn by the *Stabsschwarm* at Kristiansand-Kjevik in April giving way to a more effective overall dapple on the *Gruppen-Adjutant's* machine later in the campaign

But such was the frequency, if not the individual strengths, of the enemy's reconnaissance incursions and bombing raids, that Hentschel's pilots were nevertheless able to take a steady toll of their numbers. On 15 April they downed a pair of Hudsons, and nine days later two more Lockheed bombers plus a Blenheim. One of the two No 110 Sqn Blenheims shot down on 30 April was piloted by Sqn Ldr K C Doran who, as a flight lieutenant, had led the squadron on the first RAF bombing raid of the war over the Schillig Roads on 4 September 1939.

Although Doran, alone of his crew, survived to become a PoW, his victor, Leutnant Heinz Demes of 4.*Staffel*, was killed less than three hours later attacking two Wellington bombers. Taking hits, Demes' blazing Bf 109 was seen to dive vertically into the sea from some 80-100 metres, but not before his wingman, Oberfeldwebel Erwin Sawallisch, had claimed one of the Wellingtons (his first, incidentally, since the two he had destroyed on 14 December over the German Bight).

With II./JG 77 now even more thinly stretched from Kristiansand to

Trondheim, and with no sign of Allied air activity abating, the first single-engined fighter reinforcements had begun to appear in the shape of the Bf 109Cs and Ds of 11.(N)/JG 2. These elderly nightfighters arrived at Trondheim from Aalborg at the beginning of May, but proved too slow for the rapid-reaction scrambles and interceptions dictated by conditions in Norway. Although the nights had become very light by mid-May, and the *Staffel* flew virtually in daylight around the clock, success eluded them and they suffered a number of accidents. They transferred to Kristiansand on 21 May before returning to Germany early in June to rejoin their parent *Gruppe*.

And so, as the world's attention was firmly focussed on the *Blitzkrieg* then rolling across France and the Low Countries, Hentschel's pilots soldiered on essentially unaided and in none-too-splendid isolation. The fighting in Norway was by this time centred around the port of Narvik itself, which was too far north to allow II./JG 77 to intervene. Had they been ordered to do so, their fuel would have permitted them to remain in the area for less than five minutes.

A hare-brained scheme from on high which envisaged their arriving over Narvik and staying to destroy all the enemy's aircraft, either by ground-strafing or in combat, before themselves landing with their last drops of fuel just as the first wave of airborne troops flew in to take the field by storm was – much to their relief – dropped almost as soon as it had been suggested!

Sitting almost midway between the actions raging either side of them – Narvik to the north, the Low Countries to the south – II./JG 77 spent a relatively uneventful May. Their bag for the entire month was just two Hudsons and a single Blenheim. On 7 June King Haakon of Norway and his Government sailed to England, from where they continued the struggle. Three days later the last Norwegian troops in the far north capitulated and the ground fighting came to an end. Measured within the strict parameters of the land war, the Norwegian campaign thus did not produce a Bf 109 ace, Feldwebel Robert Menge coming closest – the Hudson he claimed on 30 May was his third victory in Norway.

But the end of the war on the ground did not herald any slackening of aerial activity. Quite the reverse. The RAF would, in fact, be stepping up its efforts to harass German coastal traffic in Norwegian waters, and to monitor and attack enemy naval units seeking sanctuary in Norway's harbours and steep-sided fjords. Within 24 hours of General Ruge's surrender, a *Schwarm* of 4./JG 77 had intercepted a dozen Hudsons of No 269 Sqn attacking the damaged battle-cruiser *Scharnhorst* at Trondheim and claimed two of their number.

Two days later, on 13 June, an even more ambitious strike – a combined operation by the RAF and the Fleet Air Arm – was launched against the *Scharnhorst*, but it went badly wrong. A raid by Coastal Command Beauforts on Trondheim-Vaernes airfield did little material damage and served mainly to alert the defending fighters. These (the Bf 109s of 4./JG 77 plus the Bf 110s of a *Zerstörerstaffel*) scrambled to give chase only to find themselves confronted by 14 unescorted Skua dive-bombers of Nos 800 and 803 Sqns FAA, launched some two hours earlier from the aircraft carrier *Ark Royal*.

The unwieldy, bomb-laden Skuas did not stand a chance. Half of them were shot down, with 4./JG 77 claiming five in just three minutes. The pair which fell to Feldwebel Robert Menge made him the first of the Norwegian-area aces. Another gave Oberfeldwebel Sawallisch his fifth too, although in the latter's case the opening three had been scored over the German Bight.

The Skuas' gallant but disastrous attack – the only bomb which hit the *Scharnhorst* failed to explode – signalled the end of the dive-bomber in Fleet Air Arm service. Against determined fighter attack it was simply too vulnerable – a lesson that was soon to be learnt by the Luftwaffe's Ju 87s in the summer skies of southern England.

While the FAA retired to lick its wounds, the RAF continued its offensive. On 15 June No 233 Sqn lost three more Hudsons near Stavanger. Two of them provided the first kills for Oberfeldwebel Anton 'Toni' Hackl, a future ace who would end the war as *Geschwaderkommodore* of JG 11, wearing the Swords to his Oak Leaves, with a final total of 192 victories. Hackl got a Beaufort six days later, one of nine No 42 Sqn machines sent to attack the *Scharnhorst* as she made her way south to home waters. Three more pilots scored against the Beauforts (which they wrongly identified as Herefords) in this action north of Bergen, including another for the indefatigable Menge and a first for Leutnant Horst Carganico, a subsequent 60-victory *Experte*.

21 June also saw the first claim in Norway by II.(J)/186, although Oberleutnant Hans Schopper's Sunderland was, in fact, only damaged. This *Gruppe* had arrived in the region at the beginning of the month, direct from action over Dunkirk. Still commanded by Hauptmann Heinrich Seeliger, II.(J)/186 was intended to bolster the coastal defences between Oslo and Trondheim. In the event, it saw little action. But exactly one month after Schopper's mistakenly claiming to have destroyed a Sunderland, Oberleutnant Lorenz Weber did succeed in shooting down one of the big 'boats – an aircraft of No 204 Sqn out to reconnoitre the Trondheim area on 21 July – only to be posted missing himself, presumed drowned in the sea, immediately following the engagement.

It was during the *Gruppe*'s eight-week sojourn in Norway that work on the Kriegsmarine's only aircraft carrier, the *Graf Zeppelin*, which had begun as long ago as 1935, was drastically slowed due to further production difficulties. It was now tacitly acknowledged that II.(J)/186, formed back in 1938 as the *Jagdgruppe* specifically intended for service aboard the vessel, faced continuing uncertainty about its future deployment. The decision was therefore taken to incorporate it into *Jagdgeschwader* 77. And it was as III./JG 77 that Seeliger's *Gruppe* departed Norway at the end of June for Berlin, where a rude shock awaited them – for the defence of the capital they were to be re-equipped with ex-French Hawk H-75As! Fortunately only 7.*Staffel* suffered this indignity, and then only for six weeks. But it was said that when the last Hawk had been handed over to a training school, the collective sigh of relief could have inflated every barrage balloon in Greater Berlin! JG 77 were to notch up a unique 'double' when II.*Gruppe* later converted to the Macchi C.205 for a brief period during the campaign in Italy. As far as is known, this makes them the only operational *Jagdgeschwader* to have flown two different types of foreign fighters on active service.

Meanwhile, II./JG 77 was continuing to protect Norway's south-western coastline against the Blenheims and Hudsons from across the North Sea. But their greatest success in southern Scandinavia was achieved not over Norwegian waters but in Denmark. 5./JG 77 had transferred from Stavanger down to Aalborg on 12 August. The following day has since gone down in history as *'Adlertag'*, or 'Eagle Day', the commencement of the Luftwaffe's all-out attack on RAF airfields at the height of the Battle of Britain.

But the bombers over England on 13 August were not all incoming. Two flights of Blenheims of No 82 Sqn – 12 aircraft in all – took off from their bases near Norwich to bomb the airfield at Aalborg in northern Jutland. One turned back on reaching the Danish coast because of fuel problems, but the other eleven continued north-eastwards across the peninsula on a direct course for their objective where, alerted by their long overland approach (the result of a navigational error), two *Schwärme* of 5./JG 77 had been scrambled to await their arrival. Every single Blenheim was shot down – five in the vicinity of the airfield, the remaining six scattered in an arc to the north-west as they attempted to escape their pursuers. The defending fighters claimed fifteen victories, the first four over the target area itself being credited to Feldwebel Robert Menge.

II./JG 77 were to remain in the north for three more months. In that time they accounted for another 15 or 16 intruders, mainly Hudsons and Blenheims. The first of these was a Blenheim brought down by Leutnant Heinrich Setz south of Stavanger on 27 August, marking the start of a combat career which would see him get 137 more victories, the Oak Leaves and command of I./JG 27 before his death in action against Spitfires over Abbeville in March 1943.

The *Gruppe* also effected a change in command during this period. Hauptmann Karl Hentschel had taken over from Major Harry von Bülow-Bothkamp just prior to the campaign in Norway when the latter was promoted to *Kommodore* of JG 2 'Richthofen'. But for some undisclosed reason Hentschel's face did not fit. And in September he was posted to a staff job after the *Staffelkapitäne* had made a unified representation direct to *Luftflotte* HQ and succeeded in obtaining his removal, despite talk of mutiny and threats of court-martial. Thus it was under the leadership of Hauptmann Franz-Heinz Lange that II./JG 77 finally departed the Scandinavian scene in mid-November 1940 when they exchanged the North Sea coastline for that of the Atlantic by taking up residence at Brest.

The *Gruppe* had scored 79 victories during its time in Norway and Denmark for the loss of six of their pilots in combat. And again one name stands out above the rest. Whatever the correct apportioning of kills over Aalborg on 13 August, Feldwebel Robert Menges' total of 13 claims undoubtedly makes him the most successful fighter pilot of the entire campaign. With four victories already achieved in Spain, he would subsequently transfer to JG 26 and fly as wingman to Oberstleutnant Adolf Galland – of which more later.

THE *BLITZKRIEG* COMES OF AGE

Bf 109E Units in the West, 10/5/40

Luftflottenkommando 2 (Northern Sector) HQ: Münster

		Base	Est-Serv
VIII. Fliegerkorps (Grevenbroich)			
Stab JG 27	Oberstlt Max. Ibel	München-Gladbach	4-4
I./JG 27	Hptm Helmut Riegel	München-Gladbach	39-28
I./JG 1	Hptm Joachim Schlichting	Gymnich	46-24
I./JG 21	Hptm Fritz Werner Ultsch	München-Gladbach	46-34
Jafü 'Deutsche Bucht' [Fighter-leader 'German Bight'] (Jever)			
Stab JG 1	Oberstlt Carl Schumacher	Jever	4-4
II.(J)/TrGr.186	Hptm Heinrich Seeliger	Wangerooge	48-35
I.(J)/LG 2	Hptm Hanns Trübenbach	Wyck (Föhr)	32-22
II./JG 2	Hptm Wolfgang Schellmann	Nordholz	47-35
IV.(N)/JG 2*	Maj Albert Blumensaat	Hopsten	31-30
*still equipped with Bf 109D			
Jafü 2 (Dortmund)			
Stab JG 26	Maj Hans Hugo Witt	Dortmund	4-3
II./JG 26	Hptm Herwig Knüppel	Dortmund	47-36
III./JG 26	Maj Ernst Freiherr von Berg	Essen-Mühlheim	42-22
III./JG 3	Hptm Walter Kienitz	Hopsten	37-25
Stab JG 51	Oberst Theo Osterkamp	Bönninghardt	4-3
I./JG 51	Hptm Hans-Heinrich Brustellin	Krefeld	47-38
I./JG 20	Hptm Hannes Trautloft	Bönninghardt	48-36
I./JG 26	Hptm Gotthardt Handrick	Bönninghardt	44-35
II./JG 27	Hptm Werner Andres	Bönninghardt	43-33
			613-447

Luftflottenkommando 3 (Southern Sector) HQ: Bad Orb

		Base	Est-Serv
I. Fliegerkorps (Cologne)			
Stab JG 77	Oberstlt Eitel Roediger von Manteuffel	Peppenhoven	4-3
I./JG 77	Hptm Johannes Janke	Odendorf	46-28
I./JG 3	Hptm Günther Lützow	Vogelsang	48-38

V. Fliegerkorps (Gersthofen)

Stab JG 52	Maj Merhart von Berneg	Mannheim-Sandhofe	3-3
I./JG 52	Hptm Siegfried von Eschwege	Lachen-Speyerdorf	46-33
II./JG 52	Hptm Hans Günther von Kornatzki	Speyer	42-28
Stab JG 54	Maj Martin Mettig	Böblingen	4-4
I./JG 54	Hptm Hubertus von Bonin	Böblingen	42-27
II./JG 51	Hptm Günther Matthes	Böblingen	42-30

Jafü 3 (Wiesbaden)

Stab JG 2	Oberstlt Harry von Bülow-Bothkamp	Frankfurt-Rebstock	4-4
I./JG 2	Hptm Roth	Frankfurt-Rebstock	45-33
III./JG 2	Hptm Dr Erich Mix	Frankfurt-Rebstock	42-11
I./JG 76	Oberstlt Richard Kraut	Ober-Olm	46-39
Stab JG 53	Oberstlt Hans-Jürgen von Cramon-Taubadel	Wiesbaden-Erbenheim	4-4
I./JG 53	Hptm Lothar von Janson	Wiesbaden-Erbenheim	46-33
II./JG 53	Hptm Günther von Maltzahn	Wiesbaden-Erbenheim	45-37
III./JG 53	Hptm Werner Mölders	Wiesbaden-Erbenheim	44-33
III./JG 52	Hptm Wolf Heinrich von Houwald	Mannheim-Sandhofen	48-39

			601-427

In contrast to the single *Jagdgruppe* which had been deemed sufficient for the subjugation of Norway, the build up of forces in the west for the forthcoming invasion of France and the Low Countries resulted, for the first time, in practically the whole of the Luftwaffe's single-engined fighter strength being brought together in one campaign. The only absentees were II./JG 77 and two detached *Staffeln* in Scandinavia, plus the *Stab* and II./JG 3 which had been held back for the defence of Berlin.

In all, 27 *Jagdgruppen* were ranged along the length of the *Westwall*, divided almost equally between *Luftflotten* 2 and 3. They were controlled by 9 *Stäbe*, not always that of their own parent *Geschwader*, which makes for the rather complicated Order of Battle shown left and above.

Of the 1000+ pilots involved, many would achieve the status of five-victory acedom in the six-week campaign that was to follow, and even more would score the first kill setting them on the road to that figure and well beyond to as-yet undreamt of heights. Space precludes their all being mentioned here, but long before France fell a number of personalities and future 'greats' were already beginning to emerge from the throng.

Briefly, the campaign itself fell into two parts, code-named *Yellow* and *Red*. Operation *Yellow* was to be initiated by an all-out attack on Holland and Belgium. This was planned to draw the British Expeditionary Force and the French northern armies to the aid of the Low Countries. Once the former were out of their prepared positions and on the move north-eastwards, the major thrust would be launched to their rear, the main *Panzer* force sweeping around behind them and driving hard for the Channel coast. Thus cut off, the Low Countries and the entrapped Anglo-French divisions could be defeated separately before the Wehrmacht wheeled about and embarked upon Operation *Red* – the advance south and west across the Somme into the heart of France.

This plan of attack meant that it was the *Jagdgruppen* of *Luftflotte* 2 to the north which were most involved at the outset, in particular those

under the command of Max Ibel's *Stab* JG 27. They formed the fighter component of *Generalmajor* von Richthofen's spearheading VIII. *Fliegerkorps*, whose Stukas, Dorniers and Henschels were tasked with breaching the Belgian and Dutch border defences.

At 21.55 hours on 9 May *Luftflotte* 2 HQ sent a brief signal to all units – 'Implement 05.35 hours'. In fact, it was 25 minutes short of that time when the first paratroop-laden Ju 52s, screened by Ibel's Bf 109s, crossed the German border north of Aachen. For on this opening day of the campaign in the west, JG 27's *Gruppen* were to be committed primarily to the protection of the tri-motored transports as they shuttled back and forth between their bases around Cologne and the airborne troops' dropping and landing zones along the Albert Canal.

It was on the very first of these missions that they claimed their first kill when I./JG 21's Hauptmann Ultsch pounced upon a solitary Belgian biplane (identified as a Firefly but more likely a Fox) patrolling north of Maastricht. Before the day was out four Belgian Gladiators had been added to the list, one falling to Leutnant Hans-Ekkehard Bob, a future 59-victory ace who would end the war flying the Me 262 in Generalleutnant Adolf Galland's JV 44.

On 11 May, freed of their close escort duties with the Ju 52s, the *Gruppen* carried out a number of *Freie Jagd* sweeps with the object of establishing local air superiority to the west of Maastricht. This brought them into conflict with not just the Belgian Air Force, but also the Low Countries' new-found Anglo-French allies, and resulted in a host of claims. Among those scoring firsts this day were the likes of Franzisket, Homuth and Redlich – all future Knight's Cross recipients. But it would prove to be the trio of Gladiators, plus a French Morane, brought down by Hauptmann Wilhelm Balthasar of I./JG 1, already with seven *Condor Legion*

A Bf 109E of I./JG 1 (the later III./JG 27) shares a forward field with the Henschel Hs 123 ground-assault biplanes of Hauptmann Weiss' II.(Schl.)/LG 2

kills to his credit, which heralded the rise of the campaign's brightest star.

Twenty-four hours later the RAF launched its near suicidal attack on the Maastricht bridges, which was to result in that service's first VCs of the war when all five of the No 12 Sqn Battles involved were shot down by a lethal combination of Flak and I./JG 27's fighters. 12 May also saw I./JG 1 bring down seven Blenheims of No 139 Sqn (including the aircraft which had carried out the RAF's first operational sortie of the war over Wilhelmshaven on 3 September 1939), before going on to destroy sixteen Belgian machines on the ground at Diest. In addition, I./JG 21 and I./JG 27 claimed eight Hurricanes between them.

Two aircraft of Max Ibel's *Geschwaderstab* were aloft that day too. Flying them were the Adjutant and the Technical Officer, the former being none other than Hauptmann Adolf Galland, arguably the most famous wartime Luftwaffe fighter pilot of them all, and certainly the best known since. Galland had flown the Heinkel He 51 in Spain, where he had been engaged primarily in ground-strafing sorties. This had led upon his return to his being posted – not back to fighters – but to the ground-attack Henschel Hs 123 *Gruppe* for the campaign in Poland.

But immediately thereafter he sought out a doctor friend in the medical branch. Displaying the resourcefulness which would see him in such good stead – not just during three years of combat flying but also through his, if anything, even more fraught term of office as *General der Jagdflieger* under an increasingly irrational and irascible Hermann Göring – Galland complained of a touch of rheumatism. The acquiescent MO had just the right remedy – 'No more open-cockpit flying'.

And so here Galland was, in his natural element, at the controls of a Bf 109E seven kilometres west of Liège, at a height of some 4000 metres with a formation of eight unsuspecting Hurricanes 1000 metres below him. Betraying his eagerness, he opened fire at alomst maximum range, but nonetheless succeeded in hitting his chosen target, which made a clumsy attempt at evasion. But a second pass sealed its fate and the Hurricane went down out of control, shedding part of its wings as it did so.

'They came from the sun with altitude advantage and I never saw them. Suddenly there was a shattering noise and the cockpit was full of burnt cordite.' This was how Sgt Frank Howell of No 87 Sqn later described the action in which he became Galland's first victim. The latter had the following to say about it;

'My first kill was child's play. An excellent weapon and luck had been on my side. To be successful, the best fighter pilot needs both.'

Eager to add to his score, Galland chased after the scattered formation and despatched another at low level – Canadian Flg Off Jack Campbell was killed in the subsequent crash – and claimed a third later that day over Tirlemont. His wingman, the same Gustav Rödel who had opened his scoreboard with I./JG 21 in the first day's fighting over Poland, being credited with a fourth. Galland long believed that his opponents had been Belgian, but that nation's small force of Hurricanes had all been caught and destroyed on the ground in the first 48 hours without seeing combat.

While Ibel's *Gruppen* had undoubtedly experienced most of the action over the Low Countries to date, the two *Jagdgeschwader* assigned to *Jafü* 2 had not been entirely inactive. Flying ahead of the first waves of the airborne divisions' Ju 52s, Major Witt's JG 26 accounted for five Dutch

Karl Borris, pictured here as a
Hauptmann, flew with JG 26 from
1940 until 1945 – for the last two
years he served as *Gruppenkommandeur* of I./JG 26

fighters on 10 May for the temporary loss of one of their own pilots who force-landed to spend the remainder of the brief campaign in the Netherlands 'having the time of his life' as a combat paratrooper.

On the second day II. and III./JG 26 clashed with French Hawk H-75As over Belgium – further proof, if any were needed, that Anglo-French forces were indeed reacting according to plan – and claimed six shot down with several others damaged. Forty-eight hours later, on 13 May, JG 26 had their final brush with the Dutch and their first with the British. Oberleutnant Karl Ebbighausen, *Staffelkapitän* of 4./JG 26, brought down the last operational Fokker T-V medium bomber of the Dutch Air Force, together with one of its two escorting G-Ia twin-engined fighters near Dordrecht. 5.*Staffel* were even more successful, encountering a fomation of six UK-based Defiants of No 264 Sqn in the same area and destroying five of them, plus one of their Spitfire escort (provided by No 66 Sqn). 5./JG 26's only loss was Leutnant Karl Borris, whose Bf 109 was hit at some 70 metres by one of the Defiants' turret gunners. Borris, who had been attending a gas-protection course in Berlin when Operation 'Yellow' was launched, had dropped everything and driven through the night back to Dortmund in time for the early morning briefing of 11 May. Now he was taking to his parachute and would spend the next four days trying to get back to his *Gruppe* again. Karl Borris was to become one of the stalwarts of JG 26, remaining with the *Geschwader* until the end of the war, by which time he would be *Kommandeur* of I.*Gruppe* with a total of 43 victories to his credit.

The other *Jafü 2 Geschwader*, JG 51, was commanded by Oberst Theo Osterkamp, one of the handful of World War 1 fighter pilots who would also fly operationally in the second conflict. With 32 victories scored in the 1914-18 war, for which he had been awarded the *Pour le Mérite*, or 'Blue Max', and having commanded the Luftwaffe's premier fighter school since, 'Onkel Theo' was already a well-known and popular figure. He needed to be, for JG 51's early months had not been without incident, having already lost two *Gruppenkommandeure*. Only 72 hours after he had taken over the *Geschwader*, Major von Berg of I./JG 51 was 'promoted sideways' out of *Luftflotte* 3 (to the command of III./JG 26) after a particularly nasty accident involving a low-flying pilot and the deaths of several schoolchildren. Then, on 2 February, II.*Gruppe's* Major Ernst Burgaller, who had flown with the Richthofen *Geschwader* in World War 1, had been killed in a crash on the shores of Lake Constance due, it is believed, to propeller mechanism failure.

And when one of his younger, more inexperienced, pilots proudly reported the shooting down of an 'unidentified twin-engined reconnaissance bomber' (which turned out to be a Focke-Wulf Fw 58 'Weihe', and the personal transport of the regional *Jagdfliegerführer*, who was aboard at the time, to boot!), it says much for Osterkamp's standing that the affair was soon common knowledge throughout the *Jagdwaffe* and the source of much amusement. 'We always knew "Onkel Theo" was ambitious, but now he's started shooting down all those above him on the promotions list!' was the joke at the time.

Oberst Osterkamp was in the lead as all four of his component *Gruppen* rendezvoused over Wesel at 05.40 hours on 10 May. Their orders were to neutralise the Dutch Air Force on the ground by a series of coordinated strikes on airfields before the arrival of the incoming Ju 52s. But the *Kommodore* was out of luck. His assigned objective, Eindhoven, appeared deserted. Nor did the second of his day's missions, covering airborne landings around Rotterdam and The Hague, bring any sightings.

But on 11 May, a day of poor visibility and lowering cloud, he claimed the first of his six World War 2 victories, a twin-boom Fokker G-Ia of the Dutch Air Force which was strafing German columns advancing along the Arnhem-Amsterdam road;

'I eased gently down through the layer of cloud. Nothing to be seen. Why I chose to look down and behind me to the left I don't know, but suddenly – there! – I catch a glimpse of something. Now it's gone again. Ease off the throttle and get down lower, perhaps from ground level I can spot him against the light of the western sky. I'm now at tree-top height. And there – off to the right, not a thousand metres ahead of me – the devil, but he's fast – full throttle and after him. He obviously hasn't seen me. He's flying straight and level at some 200 metres. I begin to catch up on him – closer and closer. I'm soaked in sweat and can hardly see through my dark sun-glasses for the condensation.

'A twin-fuselage, the Dutch markings clearly visible. Now I'm just behind and below him, pull the nose up slightly – he's filling my sights – and press all four gun buttons. All I can see are pieces flying off him, he rears up to the left and then plunges into the ground like a comet. My God, is that it? I feel he ought to be still in front of me, I had hardly fired a round. I circle. There, in the hedge alongside the road, a heap of debris, and more strewn all over the countryside – a wheel here, an engine, bits of wing and fuselage. When I think of the last war, coming back to base on one occasion with "only" 68 bullet holes in my bird–- a quick canvas patch, with a roundel and a date painted on each, and then it was back up into the fray again. But today, one hit and it's all over. We're using "cannons to shoot at sparrows!"'

'Sparrow' or not, Osterkamp's G-Ia meant that he could now add the Iron Cross, Second Class, to his 'Blue Max'.

Perhaps the least known of all Luftwaffe operations over the Low Countries were those on the far right flank of the attacking forces where Carl Schumacher's German Bight veterans were responsible for clearing the coastal belt. But they too were in action from the start, with II.(J)/186 claiming no fewer than eight Fokker D-XXIs on 10 May. One of these provided the first kill for Oberfeldwebel Kurt 'Kuddel' Ubben, a future

Dietrich Robitzsch's 'Black 1' sits forlornly on the grass at De Kooy. Note his personal marking *Der Alte* ('The Old Man') just visible beneath the cockpit

Hauptmann Heinz Bretnütz, by late 1940 *Gruppenkommandeur* of II./JG 53, is seen wearing the Knight's Cross and full overwater rig of lifejacket and a high-visibility yellow helmet cover

110-victory *Experte* and Oak Leaves recipient. Another pair were felled by Unteroffizier Herbert Kaiser, also of 5. *Staffel* but who, unlike Ubben, would survive the war, ending it with 68 kills, the Knight's Cross and latterly flying the Me 262 with Galland's JV 44. Kaiser was almost disparaging about his earliest opponents, '. . . this fixed-gear monoplane, some 75 kph slower than our Bf 109Es, offered no particular challenge'.

But his *Staffelkapitän,* Oberleutnant Dietrich Robitzsch, would perhaps have begged to differ. He was brought down during the same melée with the D-XXIs over their De Kooy base and force-landed right in the middle of the Dutch airfield. Robitzsch's war in the west had lasted less than five minutes. His time as a PoW in Canada would be measured in the same number of years and more . . . no particular challenge, indeed!

With much of the Anglo-French ground strength in the north-east irrevocably committed in the Low Countries, it was now time to launch the major armoured thrust to their immediate rear. Although relatively little activity took place in *Luftflotte* 3's area for the first day or two, 12 May did see the second member of JG 53 reach his number five, with Oberleutnant Heinz Bretnütz, *Staffelkapitän* of 6./JG 53, claiming a Potez 63 at midday. It also provided the world's third highest-scoring fighter pilot with the first of his 275 victories when Leutnant Günther Rall of 8./JG 52 downed a Hawk H-75A.

By 13 May, however, *Heeresgruppe* A's seven *Panzer* divisions had erupted out of the 'impenetrable' Ardennes and were racing for the River Meuse. To prevent their forcing this vital barrier before the French 9th Army was in place to defend it, Anglo-French bomber forces threw everything they had into destroying the Meuse river bridges at, and around, Sedan. The Luftwaffe replied in kind to prevent the destruction of these vital arteries, which would give the German tanks access to the flat plains of Picardy and beyond to the English Channel. The following 24 hours have entered Luftwaffe folklore as the 'Day of the Fighters'.

The action over Sedan saw JG 53 fully committed for the first time in the Battle of France. It was perhaps fitting that the *Jagdgeschwader* which had done more than any other to defend the integrity of Germany's border in the preceding months should now be the main instrument in securing a breach in her enemy's frontier. I./JG 53 alone claimed 13 of the 33 RAF Battles lost that day, and 10 of the 14 Blenheims destroyed. While I. *Gruppe* engaged the bombers, Werner Mölders' III./JG 53 carried out a series of *Freie Jagd* sweeps, netting seven fighters, including the *Kommandeur's* tenth. Altogether, the *Geschwader* claimed a grand total of 43.

Not surprisingly, a number of later well-known names scored their firsts over, and around, Sedan that day, future *Experten* Franz Götz and Wolfgang Tonne being just two. But the accolade must surely go to Oberleutnant Hans-Karl Mayer, *Staffelkapitän* of 1./JG 53, who already had eight Spanish victories and three World War 2 kills under his belt. The two Battles, two Blenheims and single Hurricane which he claimed on 14 May earned him pride of place among the select band of 'five-in-one day' western front aces.

By the day's end *Luftflotte* 3's fighters had flown 814 individual sorties over the bridgeheads. The remains of 89 Allied bombers and fighters lay scattered along the Meuse. Of the 71 RAF bombers which had taken off, 40 failed to return – the highest rate of loss for an operation of its size ever suffered by the RAF. In the early hours of 15 May French Prime Minister Paul Reynaud telephoned his counterpart in London. 'We are beaten', he told Winston Churchill, who had been Prime Minister of Great Britain for all of five days, 'we have lost the battle at Sedan'. Less than a week later the first German *Panzers* reached the Channel coast.

With the back of the RAF's bomber force in France effectively broken, and the Armée de l'Air in terminal disarray, there now began not just the dash for the Channel ports, but also the race for supremacy among the Luftwaffe's top-scoring pilots. Werner Mölders was still in the lead – a position he consolidated the day after Sedan by claiming his eleventh, one of three Hurricanes downed by the *Stabsschwarm* of III./JG 53.

But other names were beginning to be heard. That 15 May also witnessed the fifth victory of Hauptmann Gunther Lützow, and the fiftieth for his *Gruppe*, I./JG 3 – 24 hours later Adolf Galland of JG 27 claimed a Spitfire near Lille. This was the day that JG 26 first appeared over France as the fighters of *Luftflotte* 2, freed from the Low Countries by the capitulation of the Netherlands on 14 May, began to add their weight to the main push in the south.

But the drive to the coast was not without its casualties. On 18 May 7./JG 53 lost their *Staffelkapitän* when Oberleutnant Wolf-Dietrich Wilcke baled out over French territory after his aircraft was hit in a dogfight with Hawk H-75As. The next day Hauptmann Herwig Knüppel, *Kommandeur* of II./JG 26, was shot down over Lille. On 21 May another World War 1 veteran, Hauptmann Dr Erich Mix, *Gruppenkommandeur* of III./JG 2, was bested in a duel with 'Morane' fighters and forced to land behind enemy lines. Hiding up by day and moving by night, he returned to his unit 48 hours later, and subsequently added 13 victories to the three

An *Emil* of II./JG 53 at Charleville in May 1940. Note the transitionary combination of definitive fuselage cross with centre-line tail Swastika – also the remains of what appears to be a Belgian Fairy Fox in the foreground

47

he scored during the 1914-18 conflict.

And so it went on – a growing list of victories on the one hand, offset by fatalities or capture by the enemy on the other. But for the survivors of those heady days of May-June 1940, the abiding memories are not just of the aerial skirmishes, but perhaps even more of the confusion and chaos that accompanied their constant moves forward from one bomb-cratered enemy airfield, or unprepared landing strip, to the next as they sought desperately to keep pace with the advancing ground forces. It was a situation no amount of peacetime manoeuvres could have prepared them for, and nearly every one of them has a story to tell.

Members of 8./JG 2 relax at Signy-le-Petit now that the woods in the background have been cleared of French Army stragglers! The pilot on the right is Feldwebel Willinger who, six months later over the Channel, would score JG 2's 500th victory of the war

Take the pilot of JG 2, for example, who was ordered to scout ahead for a suitable site and who laid claim to an airfield near Charleville, only to be usurped by the arrival in numbers of JG 27. Forced to move to nearby Signy-le-Petit, he was warned that the area was still alive with French troops. Taking ten men to comb the woods bordering the field, he ended up by capturing a corps commander, three divisional generals and 200 French colonial soldiers. Discretion being the better part of valour, the 11 dismantled a pair of machine-guns from the wreckage of one of the many French Potez aircraft littering the tiny field and barricaded themselves for the night in the top storey of a neighbouring farmhouse while business went on as usual below – the building doubled as the local bar and brothel! The pilots of I.(J)/LG 2 went to the other extreme; spending part of the campaign housed in a nunnery.

Nor did JG 27's *force majeure* occupation of Charleville benefit them much. Within easy range of French artillery, they soon found that supplies were hard to come by. Before long they were reduced to 'impounding' every aircraft that happened to land there on its way back to the rear. They would then syphon off its fuel, leaving just enough for it to reach the next stop on its journey. No respecter of persons, this treatment was even meted out to a visiting Ju 52 of the *Führer's* Flight!

Charleville was a busy stop-over point in the race across France for many *Jagdgruppen* including II./JG 53

More alarming still, the pilots of JG 77 had to fight to retain possession of Escarmain, beating off an attack by some 400 heavily armed French infantry to do so. And instances of Bf 109s having to land on abandoned fields between piles of debris and aircraft wrecks half hidden in grass a metre or more high are legion. One worthy, despite being greeted by a veritable firework display of red flares, carefully touched down close alongside – but

A French MS.406 abandoned at Escarmain, scene of JG 77's famous 'firefight' with attacking enemy infantry

The festivities are under way at Loe in late May in celebration of Werner Mölders winning the Knight's Cross – the first to be awarded to a member of the *Jagdwaffe*

fortunately not on top of – a row of tiny flags, thinking these marked out a clear path, only to be told that they in fact indicated the location of a stick of unexploded bombs!

But despite such alarms and excursions on the ground, the war in the air was drawing towards its inevitable conclusion. The scores of the budding *'Experten'* continued to mount, although Mölders' 13th, shot down on the evening of 20 May, poses something of a mystery. Even to somebody who apparently found it difficult to differentiate between a Hawk and a Hurricane in the heat of combat, the distinctive silhouette of a Vickers Wellesley – for such was the type of aircraft claimed destroyed – should have been unmistakable. But the actual identity of the victim remains unknown – was it the single Fairey Battle listed as missing that day, or did Werner Mölders really encounter a Wellesley overflying France en route from the UK to East Africa?

With the evacuation of the RAF Component from France on 22 May the stage was set for the final act of Operation *Yellow*. The following day JG 27 were over the Channel ports protecting Bf 110 *Zerstörer* units from attack by UK-based fighters (shades of things to come!), during the course of which they claimed 18 victories in the Calais-Dunkirk area, including 3 to Hauptmann Balthasar and 2 to Leutnant Franzisket, for the loss of 4 of their own. Three days later Balthasar got two more Spitfires over Calais. 2./JG 2 were also heading for Calais on that 26 May, escorting Ju 87 Stukas on their way to bomb the last defenders out of the port's Citadel. Encountering a force of some 20 Spitfires (from Nos 19 and 65 Sqns), the *Staffel* shot down five .

But it was Mölders' downing two Hawk H-75As south of Amiens the following morning which brought his score to 20 and resulted in the award of the Knight's Cross two days later. Hauptmann Werner Mölders was the first Luftwaffe fighter pilot to achieve this total and the first to be so honoured – an occasion that was suitably celebrated at III./JG 53's base at Loe near La Selve.

One of the many Hurricanes lost to the RAF during the retreat across France, this is believed to be an abandoned No 3 Sqn aircraft whose fuselage roundel and markings have already been stripped by souvenir hunters. Note the He 111 bomber on the left and Ju 52 transports in the background on the right-hand side

A fresh-faced Josef Priller serving with the *Stabsschwarm* I./JG 51 in the opening weeks of the war. He would score his first 20 kills with JG 51 before going on to greater glory – by adding another 81 – with JG 26, the *Geschwader* with which his name is inextricably linked (see *Aircraft of the Aces 9*)

Belgium had finally capitulated in the early hours of 28 May and by now the British evacuation from Dunkirk was in full swing. The number of claims made by the Luftwaffe's *Jagdgruppen* above the beaches of Dunkirk in the next few days effectively gives the lie to the bitter criticism voiced at the time by many in the BEF that '. . . the RAF was nowhere to be seen'.

On 28 May the three *Gruppen* of JG 26 had shot down 15 British fighters in the area, including 6 Spitfires which fell to Major Handrick's I./JG 26 during a violent confrontation in the immediate vicinity of the evacuation beaches, and 6 Hurricanes downed by III./JG 26 just along the coast over Ostend. Twenty-four hours later Adolf Galland landed back at St Pol, his aircraft covered in oil, claiming a Blenheim shot into the sea (although this may have been the badly damaged No 21 Sqn aircraft which made it back to its own base for a wheels-up landing).

Among the 65(!) other aircraft destroyed by the Luftwaffe that 29 May were 10 downed by I.(J)/LG 2 alone – 8 Hurricanes over Dunkirk and a brace of MS.406s inland near St Quentin. One of each of these provided firsts for future aces - a Hurricane shot down by Leutnant Friedrich-Wilhelm Strakeljahn (a later luminary in the ranks of the ground-attack arm), and one of the Moranes which was claimed by Oberleutnant Herbert Ihlefeld, who would be wearing the Swords and have 130 victories to his credit by war's end.

Many more names – some already familiar, others soon to be so – made their mark over Dunkirk with multiple victories. Osterkamp, Priller and Oesau, all of JG 51, each claimed three apiece. Joachim Müncheberg, *Gruppen-Adjutant* of III./JG 26, went one better with four kills, all scored on 31 May. Next day JG 27 downed two Wellingtons – one by Feldwebel Sawallisch – to the east of the shrinking Dunkirk perimeter, plus six Spitfires, one of the latter being Adolf Galland's eleventh victory.

The Dunkirk evacuation was completed early on the morning of 3 June. By now, however, the Luftwaffe's attention had already turned elsewhere. As a preliminary to Operation *Red* – the reduction of the rest of France – a major air attack was mounted against a series of military targets in the Greater Paris area. Code-named Operation *Paula*, these Paris raids of 3 June resulted in some of the last large-scale engagements of the French campaign.

JG 53, which had not been directly involved over Dunkirk, was credited with 11 kills that day.

Hauptmann Werner Mölders, still favouring the fur-collared 'Spanish look' of his *Condor Legion* days, is seen shortly before being reported missing in action against French fighters on 5 June 1940

The tail of Wilhelm Balthasar's *Emil* (Wk-Nr 1559) displays only 3 victories more than the 36 he claimed during the Battle of France as *Kapitän* of 7./JG 27, despite this photograph's reportedly being taken over three months later (at Samer on 7 October 1940). Now promoted to *Kommandeur* of III./JG 3, Balthasar (centre) is seen here chatting to the *Kommodore* of JG 3, Major Günther Lützow (left), while the life-jacketed *Staffelkapitän* of 9./JG 3, Oberleutnant Egon Troha, looks on (right)

Wreckage of a French Amiot bomber of the type downed by Oberleutnant Walter Oesau on 13 June as JG 51's last kill of the campaign in the West

These included numbers 22 and 23 for Werner Mölders – a Hawk H-75A and a 'Spitfire' (although the latter was more likely to have been a Dewoitine D.520). And Adolf Galland claimed his 12th, a Morane MS.406, north of the French capital. I./(J)/LG 2 and II./JG 2 also participated in Operation *Paula*, scoring 6 and 12 respectively.

Forty-eight hours later the unthinkable happened. Shortly before noon on 5 June – the opening day of Operation *Red* – Werner Mölders claimed two more victims, a Bloch 152 fighter and a Potez 63 over Compiègne. Back in the air with his *Stabsschwarm* early that same evening, Mölders was about to attack a formation of six 'Moranes' when another *Staffel* dived in front of him. Opening fire much too early, they alerted the French fighters who immediately broke in all directions. A wild dogfight developed. Mölders later described what happened next;

'I watch the fight for a while and then go in to attack a Morane which is being chased – without success – by three other Messerschmitts. I soon have him in my sights – he immediately dives away, but clearly hasn't had enough yet. Suddenly he pulls up beneath me, I lose sight of him underneath my wing – there he is again, below me off to one side – *Donnerwetter!* This Morane can shoot too, although he's well wide of the mark.

'I bank away and climb up into the sun. He must have lost me, for he banks in the opposite direction and disappears to the south. Beneath me two Messerschmitts are still having a go at the last Morane.

'A glance above and behind me – the sky still full of weaving Me's. I am at about 800 metres – suddenly a bang and sparks fly across the cockpit. The throttle is shot to pieces, the stick flops forward. I'm going down vertically. Got to get out, otherwise it's all over . . .

'I grab the jettison lever and the canopy flies off. My faithful bird points her nose upwards for a second or two and gives me one last chance to undo my harness and clamber out of the seat. Free!'

While Werner Mölders was taking to his parachute, his opponent, Lt Pomier-Layragues of GC II/7, reportedly claimed a second Messerschmitt before himself being shot down in flames a few moments later. The identity of the pilot who so quickly avenged the loss of his *Gruppenkommandeur* has never been established, for III./JG 53's trio of victories for that evening are all listed as Moranes. And, true to form, Mölders had got it wrong again – his opponents had, in fact, been flying the new Dewoitine D.520, undoubtedly the best French fighter of the campaign.

With Werner Mölders gone, other names took over the running. JG 27 had also been active on 5 June, claiming no fewer than 22 kills north-east of Paris. Five of these were credited to Hauptmann Wilhelm Balthasar. Nine days later the *Staffelkapitän* of 7./JG 27 would become the second fighter pilot to receive the Knight's Cross, by which time his total had risen to 23. Although two short of Mölders' score, the 13 additional aircraft he

destroyed on the ground have won Balthasar recognition as the most successful fighter pilot of the campaign in the west.

The French fighter arm had been grievously mauled during the three weeks of May, but it was by no means a wholly spent force. Both it and those units of the RAF's Advanced Air Striking Force still remaining in France continued to oppose the German tide now sweeping west and south in pursuance of Operation *Red*.

13 June, for example, witnessed fierce aerial activity, with JG 27 claiming 23 aircraft destroyed, including six Battles attacking German armoured units in the Montmirail-Provins areas east of Paris, which fell to I. *Gruppe*. But the final outcome was by now beyond doubt. That same 13 June Oberleutnant Walter Oesau claimed JG 51's last French victim by downing an Amiot bomber. Two days earlier JG 53 had closed their books in France with five kills. Two of these had been MS.406s claimed by Hauptmann Rolf Pingel, which brought his personal tally to six. Other future Knight's Cross holders scored their firsts during this period, Günther Seeger of JG 2 and Alfred Heckmann and Georg Schentke of JG 3, all beginning their rise to acedom early in June.

The Maginot Line was finally breached near Saarbrücken on 15 June,

Emils of III./JG 26 undergoing maintenance at Villacoublay in June 1940 after the rigours of the previous weeks' fighting. Note too that the early style narrow-bordered fuselage crosses have been partially oversprayed preparatory to new ones being applied

Heavily mottled Bf 109E 'White 2' of 1./JG 3 revels in the *Jagdwaffe's* newly won supremacy of the French Channel coast as it soars above the chalk cliffs near Wissant in the Pas de Calais

and a week later the Armistice was signed at Compiègne, with elements of both JGs 26 and 53 providing a symbolic aerial umbrella over the proceedings. The Cease Fire sounded at 00.35 hours on 25 June.

By this time the bulk of the *Jagdwaffe* was already heading back to Germany to rest, recuperate and refit. Göring was in no hurry to take the fight across the Channel, preferring instead to let his pilots rest upon their laurels after the magnificent victory just won over France. Only one *Jagdgeschwader,* Oberst Osterkamp's JG 51, was moved up into the Pas de Calais across the straits from England. It would thus fall to 'Onkel Theo's' pilots to launch the Bf 109E into the next (and arguably most famous) chapter of its operational history, for although the Battle of France may have been over, the Battle of Britain had yet to be won.

COLOUR PLATES

This 12–page section profiles many of the aircraft flown by the *Jagdwaffe's* first aces of World War 2. All the artwork has been specially commissioned for this volume, and author/profile artist John Weal and figure artist Mike Chappell have gone to great pains to illustrate the aircraft and their pilots as accurately as possible following in-depth research. Many of the Bf 109s depicted over the following pages have never been illustrated before, and the schemes shown have been fully authenticated by surviving pilots from the 1939/41 period.

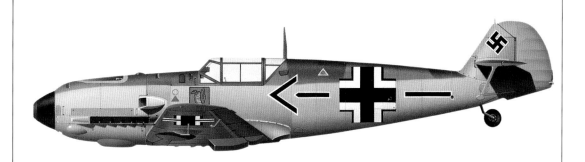

1
Bf 109E-3 'Black Chevron and Bars' of Oberstleutnant Carl Schumacher, *Geschwaderkommodore* JG 1, Jever, Spring 1940

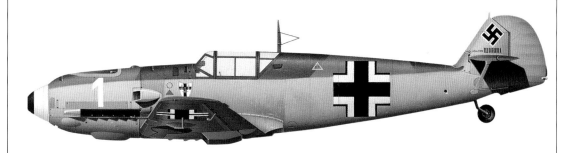

2
Bf 109E-4 (Wk-Nr 1486) 'White 1' of Hauptmann Wilhelm Balthasar, *Staffelkapitän* of 1./JG 1, Monchy-Breton, May 1940

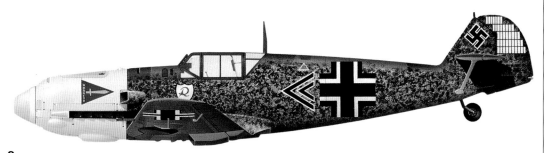

3
Bf 109E-4 (Wk-Nr 5344) 'Black Double Chevron' of Hauptmann Helmut Wick, *Gruppenkommandeur* of I./JG 2 'Richthofen', Beaumont-le-Roger, October 1940

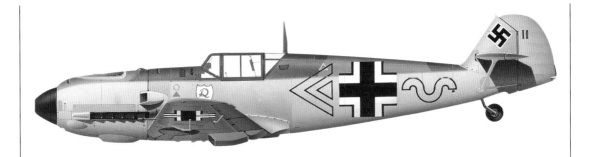

4
Bf 109E 'Chevron-Triangle' of Major Dr Erich Mix, *Gruppenkommandeur* III./JG 2 'Richthofen, France, May 1940

5
Bf 109E-4 'White 1' of Oberleutnant Werner Machold, *Staffelkapitän* 7./JG 2 'Richthofen', Le Havre, September 1940

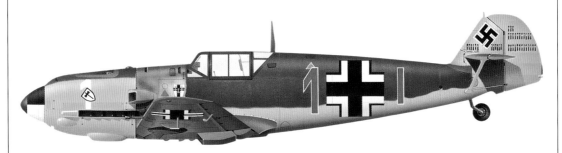

6
Bf 109E-4 (Wk-Nr 1559) 'Green 1' of Hauptmann Wilhelm Balthasar, *Gruppenkommandeur* III./JG 3, Desvres, August 1940

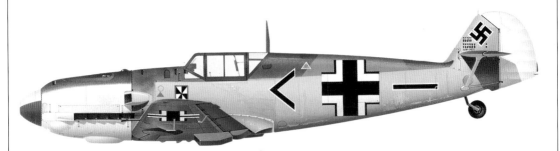

7
Bf 109E-4 (Wk-Nr 1480) 'Black Chevron' of Oberleutnant Franz von Werra, *Gruppen-Adjutant* II./JG 3, Samer, August 1940

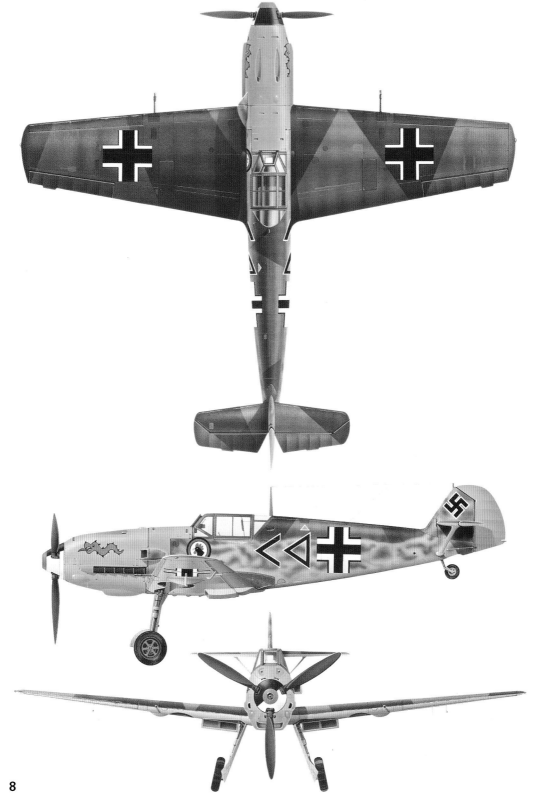

8
Bf 109E-4 'Black Chevron and Triangle' of Hauptmann Hans von Hahn, *Gruppenkommandeur* I./JG 3, Colombert, August 1940

9
Bf 109E-4 'Black Chevron-Triangle and Bar' of Hauptmann Hannes Trautloft, *Gruppenkommandeur* I./JG 20, Bönninghardt, March 1940

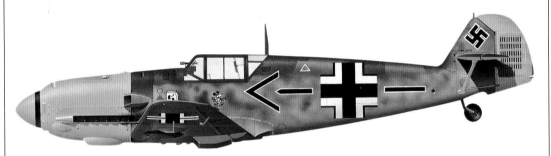

10
Bf 109E-4/N (Wk-Nr 5819) 'Black Chevron and Bars' of Oberstleutnant Adolf Galland, *Geschwaderkommodore* JG 26 'Schlageter', Audembert, December 1940

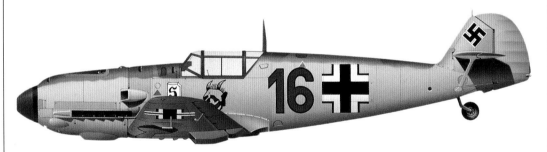

11
Bf 109E 'Red 16' of Oberleutnant Fritz Losigkeit, *Staffelkapitän* of 2./JG 26 'Schlageter', Bönninghardt, March 1940

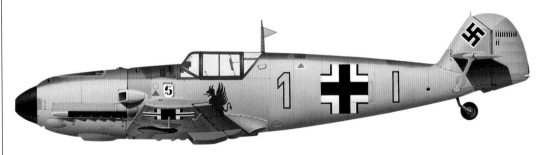

12
Bf 109E-4 'Yellow 1' of Oberleutnant Gerhard Schöpfel, *Staffelkapitän* of 9./JG 26 'Schlageter', Caffiers, August 1940

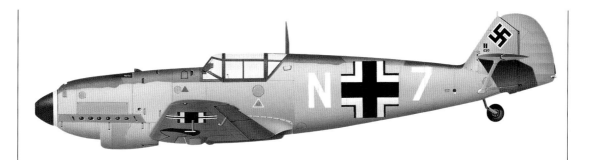

13
Bf 109D (Wk-Nr 630) 'White N7' of Oberleutnant Johannes Steinhoff, *Staffelkapitän* of 10.(N)/JG 26, Jever, December

14
Bf 109E 'Red 5' of Leutnant Josef Buerschgens, 2./JG 26 'Schlageter', Odendorf, September 1939

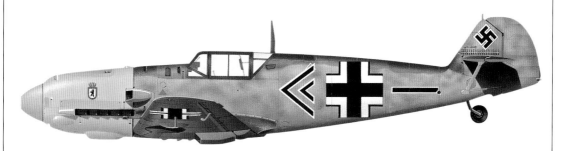

15
Bf 109E-4 'Double Chevron' of Hauptmann Wolfgang Lippert, *Gruppenkommandeur* II/JG 27, Montreuil, September 1940

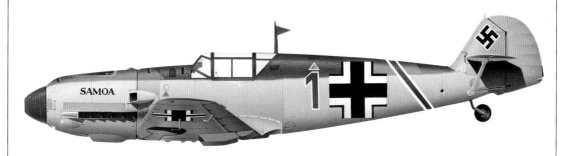

16
Bf 109E-1 'Red 1' of Oberleutnant Gerd Framm, *Staffelkapitän* 2./JG 27, Krefeld, January 1940

17
Bf 109E-1 'Black Chevron' of Oberleutnant Josef Priller, *Gruppen-Adjutant* I./JG 51, Eutingen, September 1939

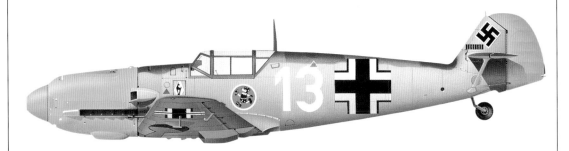

18
Bf 109E 'White 13' of Feldwebel Heinz Bär, 1./JG 51, Pihen, September 1940

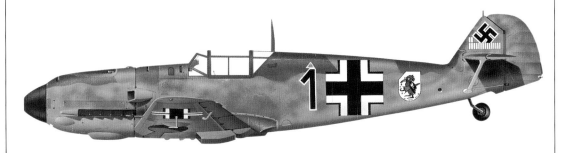

19
Bf 109E 'Black 1' of Hauptmann Horst Tietzen, *Staffelkapitän* 5./JG 51, Marquise, August 1940

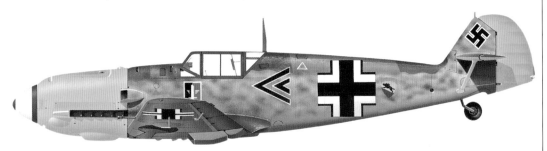

20
Bf 109E 'Black Double Chevron' of Hauptmann Wolfgang Ewald, *Gruppenkommandeur* I./JG 52, Coquelles, September 1940

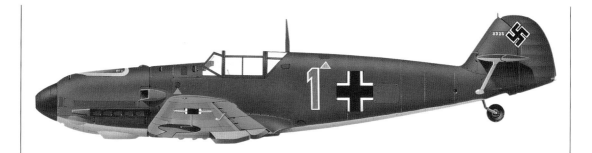

21
Bf 109E (Wk-Nr 3335) 'Red 1' of Leutnant Hans Berthel, 2./JG 52, Bonn-Hangelar, October 1939

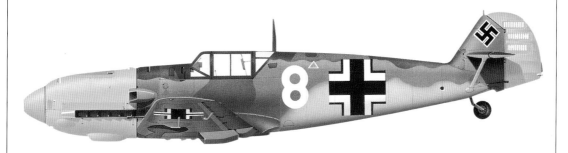

22
Bf 109E 'White 8' of Hauptmann Hans-Karl Mayer, *Gruppenkommandeur* I./JG 53 'Pik-As', Etaples, September 1940

23
Bf 109E 'Black Chevron-Triangle' of Hauptmann Werner Mölders, *Gruppenkommandeur* III./JG 53 'Pik-As', Trier-Euren, March 1940

24
Bf 109E 'Black Chevron-Triangle' of Hauptmann Harro Harder, *Gruppenkommandeur* of III./JG 53 'Pik-As', Villiaze/Guernsey, August 1940

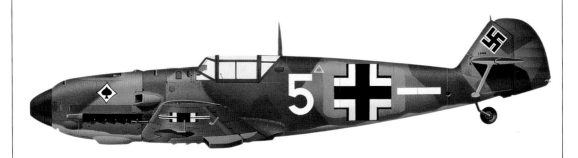

25
Bf 109E-3 (Wk-Nr 1244) 'White 5' of Unteroffizier Stefan Litjens, 4./JG 53 'Pik-As', Mannheim-Sandhofen, October 1939

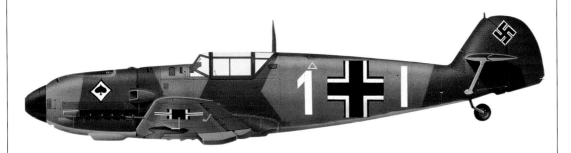

26
Bf 109E 'White 1' of Oberleutnant Wolf-Dietrich Wilcke, *Staffelkapitän* 7./JG 53 'Pik-As', Wiesbaden-Erbenheim, October 1939

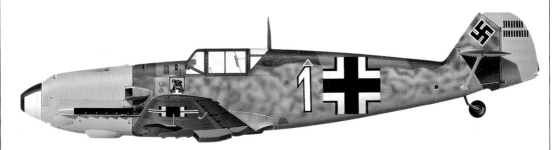

27
Bf 109E-4 'White 1' of Oberleutnant Hans Philipp, *Staffelkapitän* 4./JG 54, Hermelingen, October 1940

28
Bf 109E-4 (Wk-Nr 1572) 'Black 3' of Leutnant Erwin Leykauf, 8./JG 54, Guines-South, September 1940

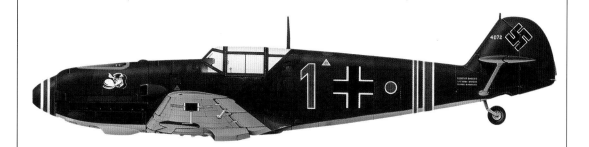

29
Bf 109E-1 (Wk-Nr 4072) 'Red 1' of Hauptmann Hannes Trautloft, *Staffelkapitän* 2./JG 77, Juliusburg, September 1939

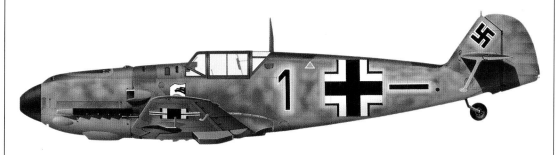

30
Bf 109E 'Black 1' of Feldwebel Robert Menge, 5./JG 77, Aalborg, August 1940

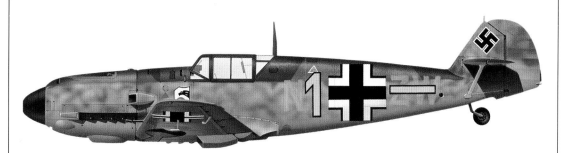

31
Bf 109E 'Yellow 1' of Oberleutnant Wilhelm Moritz, *Staffelkapitän* 6./JG 77, Kristiansand-Kjevik, September 1940

32
Bf 109E 'Yellow 11' of Feldwebel Alfred Held, 6./JG 77, Nordholz, September 1939

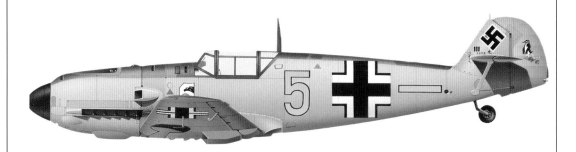

33
Bf 109E (Wk-Nr 1279) 'Yellow 5' of Feldwebel Hans Troitzsch, 6./JG 77, Wangerooge, December 1939

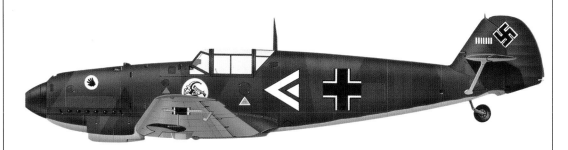

34
Bf 109D 'White Chevron-Triangle' of Hauptmann Hannes Gentzen, *Jagdgruppe* 102 (I./ZG 2), Bernburg, October 1939

35
Bf 109E 'Yellow 13' of Feldwebel Kurt Ubben, 6.(J)/TrGr.186, Wangerooge, March 1940

36
Bf 109E 'Black 1' of Oberleutnant Herbert Ihlefeld, *Gruppenkommandeur* I.(J)/LG 2, Marquise, September 1940

1
Major Werner Mölders,
Geschwaderkommodore of JG 51,
at Wissant in late September 1940

2
Major Adolf Galland,
Geschwaderkommodore of JG 26,
at Audembert in October 1940

3
Hauptmann Günther Lützow,
Gruppenkommandeur of I./JG 3,
at Grandvillers in early October 1940

4
Hauptmann Helmut Wick,
Gruppenkommandeur of I./JG 2, at
Beaumont-le-Roger in October 1940

5
Hauptmann Heinz Bretnütz,
Gruppenkommandeur of II./JG 53,
at Dinan in September 1940

6
Hauptmann Hermann-Friedrich
Joppien, *Gruppenkommandeur* of
I./JG 51, at Pihen in late August 1940

THE BATTLE OF BRITAIN AND AFTER

Bf 109E Units in the Battle of Britain, 13/8/40

Luftflottenkommando 2 HQ: Brussels

		Base	Est-Serv
II. Fliegerkorps (Ghent)			
Erpr.Gr.210[*]	*Hptm* Walter Rubensdörffer	Calais-Marck	10-9
[*](1 *Staffel* of Bf 109E-4B fighter-bombers; 2 *Staffeln* of Bf 110s)			
Jagdfliegerführer 2 (Wissant)			
Stab JG 3	Oberstlt Carl Vieck	Wierre-au-Bois	3-3
I./JG 3	Hptm Günther Lützow	Grandvillers	33-32
II./JG 3	Hptm Erich von Selle	Samer	29-22
III./JG 3	Hptm Walter Kienitz	Desvres, Le Touquet	29-29
Stab JG 26	Maj Gotthardt Handrick	Audembert	4-4
I./JG 26	Hptm Kurt Fischer	Audembert	38-34
II./JG 26	Hptm Karl Ebbighausen	Marquise-East	39-35
III./JG 26	Maj Adolf Galland	Caffiers	40-38
Stab JG 51	Maj Werner Mölders	Wissant	4-4
I./JG 51	Hptm Hans-Heinrich Brustellin	Pihen nr Calais	32-32
II./JG 51 (I./JG 71)	Hptm Günther Matthes	Marquise-West	33-33
III./JG 51 (I./JG 20)	Hptm Hannes Trautloft	St Omer-Clairmarais	32-30
Stab JG 52	Maj Merhart von Bernegg	Coquelles	2-1
I./JG 52	Hptm Siegfried von Eschwege	Coquelles	40-33
II./JG 52	Hptm Hans-Günther von Kornatzki	Peuplingues	39-32
(III./JG 52	Hptm Alexander von Winterfeld	Zerbst	31-11)
I.(J)/LG 2	Hptm Hanns Trübenbach	Calais-Marck	36-33
Stab JG 54	Maj Martin Mettig	Campagne-les-Guines	4-2
I./JG 54 (I./JG 70)	Hptm Hubertus von Bonin	Guines	34-24
II./JG 54 (I./JG 76)	Hptm Helmut Bode	Hermelingen	36-32
III./JG 54 (I./JG 21)	Hptm Fritz Werner Ultsch	Guines-South	42-40

590-513

Luftflottenkommando 3 HQ: Paris

		Base	Est-Serv
***VIII. Fliegerkorps* (Deauville)**			
II.(Schl.)/LG 2**	Maj Otto Weiss	Böblingen	39-31
**Bf 109E-7 fighter-bombers; re-equipping			
***Jagdfliegerführer 3* (Deauville)**			
Stab JG 2	Oberst Harry von Bülow-Bothkamp	Beaumont-le-Roger	3-3
I./JG 2	Hptm Hennig Strümpell	Beaumont-le-Roger	34-32
II./JG 2	Hptm Wolfgang Schellmann	Beaumont-le-Roger	36-28
III./JG 2	Maj Dr Erich Mix	Le Havre	32-28
Stab JG 27	Oberstlt Max Ibel	Cherbourg-West	5-4
I./JG 27	Hptm Eduard Neumann	Plumetôt	37-32
II./JG 27	Hptm Werner Andres	Crépon	40-32
III./JG 27 (I./JG1)	Hptm Joachim Schlichting	Arcques	39-32
Stab JG 53	Maj Hans-Jürgen von Cramon-Taubadel	Cherbourg	6-6
I./JG 53	Hptm Albert Blumensaat	Rennes, Guernsey	39-37
II./JG 53	Hptm Günther von Maltzahn	Dinan, Guernsey	38-34
III./JG 53	Hptm Wolf-Dietrich Wilcke	Brest, Sempy	38-35
			386-334

The red 'Arched cat' badge (deceptively similar to 8./JG 51's black version) seen on this camouflaged *Emil* was the emblem of 4./JG 52, whose *Staffelkapitän* was one Oberleutnant Johannes Steinhoff. After scoring 176 kills, Steinhoff was seriously wounded when his Me 262 of JV 44 crashed on take-off from München-Riem on 18 April 1945

The build-up to '*Adlertag*', the main air offensive against the United Kingdom, again witnessed – for only the second and last time in its history – practically the entire frontline strength of the Luftwaffe's single-engined fighter force being concentrated together in one area: the Channel coast. But once again JG 77 was absent, all three of its component *Gruppen* now being widely dispersed outside Berlin, along the shores of the North Sea and in Scandinavia. Before the year was out, however, two of these *Gruppen* would also be in France.

Otherwise, just about the only operational Bf 109s not to be directly involved in the Battle of Britain were Carl Schumacher's *Stabsschwarm* (which continued to guard the German Bight using an ever-changing miscellany of training units or *Jagdgruppen* either en route to, or returning from, the Channel front) and the last remaining Bf 109D and E nightfighters still operated by III./NJG 1 at Cologne-Ostheim.

The course of the Battle itself is too well known to warrant repetition here, other than where it has a direct bearing on the continuing careers of those aces already familiar from the fighting on the continent. The coming confrontation would also provide the first rung on the ladder of success for many more future *Experten*, some of whom would later number among the highest scorers in the *Jagdwaffe*. But it saw too the abrupt termination of other, equally promising, careers and the first losses among the ranks of the newly fledged Knight's Cross holders.

One thing which the four-week hiatus prior to the start of the Battle proper did provide was an opportunity to rationalise the still somewhat untidy nature of the *Jagdwaffe*'s organisation. The half-dozen *Jagdgeschwader* which had been in the

Leutnant Waldemar Wübke, seen here in front of his 'Yellow 11' of 9./JG 54, ended the war with a modest tally of 15 kills. He also served alongside Steinhoff as a member of Galland's elite JV 44 in the closing weeks at München-Riem, albeit flying Fw 190D-9s of the airfield's protection *Staffel*

process of formation upon the outbreak of war, but which had not progressed beyond the single *Gruppe* stage since, were now finally all redesignated and incorporated into existing *Geschwader* (for details see Order of Battle).

Another result of the French capitulation was the return of captured personnel. Unlike those flyers who had gone down in the early stages of the campaign over the Low Countries and had been transported to the UK (and often thence to Canada) as PoWs, those captured during Operation *Red* were mostly still in French hands. Among the returnees were JG 53's Wolf-Dietrich Wilcke and Werner Mölders.

Mölders wrote a long letter to his old *Gruppe*, III./JG 53, saying how much he was enjoying his three weeks leave and also describing his impressions after being invited by Ernst Udet, Chief of Aircraft Procurement and Supply, to fly a captured Hurricane and Spitfire at the Luftwaffe's Rechlin test centre;

'The Hurricane is a bit of a tugboat (*Jagddampfer*) with a retractable undercarriage. In our terms both are very easy to fly, the Hurricane particularly good-natured, steady as a rock in the turn, but well below the Bf 109 when it comes to performance – it's heavy on the rudder and the ailerons are sluggish. Take-off and landing of both types is child's play.

'The Spitfire is one class better, very nice to the touch, light, excellent in the turn and almost equal to the Bf 109 in performance, but a rotten dogfighter as any sudden dive and the engine cuts out for seconds at a time, and because the propeller's only two-pitch (take-off and cruise) it means that in any vertical dogfight at constantly changing heights it's either continually over-revving or never develops full power at all' – which, in the light of the events to come, makes for interesting reading.

But while most fighter units were taking it easy back in the *Reich*, cross-Channel traffic had not ceased altogether. Hauptmann Hanns Trübenach's I.(J)/LG 2 became the first *Gruppe* to 'bridge the gap' between the Battles of France and Britain. Upon the cessation of the fighting in France this *Gruppe* was one of the few not to retire to Germany, instead being stood down for 72 hours rest before being subordinated to JG 51 in the Pas de Calais.

Presumably suitably refreshed, it was they who intercepted one of the

RAF's first bombing raids across the Channel since the French surrender, bringing down three of the nine Blenheims of No 107 Sqn sent to attack Merville airfield on 30 June. Two bombers fell to Oberleutnant Herbert Ihlefeld, and the third to Oberfeldwebel Erwin Clausen. But they lost Unteroffizier Rauhut to the Blenheims' return fire. Four days later the action had switched to the other side of the Channel, with Leutnant Geisshardt's claiming of two Hurricanes of No 32 Sqn (both landed damaged) over the Kent coast for the loss of Unteroffizier Gustav Schiller.

For the first three weeks of July Oberst Theo Osterkamp's four *Gruppen* provided almost the sole fighter protection for the Luftwaffe bombers and Stukas attempting to close the Channel to British coastal convoys. This was to involve them in a whole series of skirmishes with defendng RAF fighters, and set in train the steady rate of attrition among the more inexperienced pilots which hall-marked the Battle for nearly every participating *Jagdgeschwader*. To use JG 51 as an example, of the ten pilots lost during July, half had themselves failed to score a single victory, and the remaining five had achieved just eleven between them. And this ratio was to remain remarkably constant. Of the 100 pilots lost to the *Geschwader* between July 1940 and their departure for the east in June 1941, just over half had not scored at all, and of the rest 35 had less than 5 kills. It was 'natural selection' at its harshest. If a young pilot came through his first few missions unscathed, his chances of survival – at least in the short to medium term – were immeasurably improved.

Meanwhile, the natural *Experten* continued to add to their successes. As on 10 July when III./JG 51 were part of the escort for a formation of Do 17s attacking a convoy off Dover. The other escorting fighters were the Bf 110s of I./ZG 26. And when, at the first sign of opposition, these latter immediately went into one of their ineffectual 'defensive circles' (the first cracks in the armour of the vaunted 'Ironsides' were already showing), it fell to the Bf 109s alone to protect the Dorniers. In the course of the ensuing dogfight Oberleutnant Walter Oesau, *Staffelkapitän* of 7./JG 51, claimed his first two victories of the Battle. Three days later Oberst Osterkamp got his sixth, and last, of World War 2 when he reported shooting a Spitfire into the Channel south of Dover (although, in fact, his victim was more likely to have been one of the two No 56 Sqn Hurricanes reported missing in that area).

There were no problems of recognition for III./JG 51 on 19 July when they engaged a squadron of unsuspecting Defiants patrolling off Folke-stone. Coming in from below and astern so that the Defiants' turret gun-ners could not bring their weapons to bear, Hauptmann Trautloft's pilots sent four down in flames in less than a minute. Two others were damaged

A serious looking Oberleutnant Josef Priller, now *Staffelkapitän* of 6./JG 51, briefs his pilots. On the extreme right is Herbert Huppertz who would be awarded the Oak Leaves posthumously after his death in action against P-47s over Normandy on D + 2 as *Gruppen-kommandeur* of III./JG 2

JG 2's Franz Jaenisch was the pilot who first landed among the wheat at Beaumont-le-Roger. A one-time wingman of Mölders in Spain (where he scored a solitary victory), Jaenisch commemorates that earlier conflict with his own version of the well-known *Mickey Mouse* badge. Here, he receives a congratulatory garland for completing his 100th mission . . .

. . . and the sumptuous looking villa at Beaumont which served as JG 2's combined HQ and living quarters. Deserted by its previous occupants when first taken over, Hauptmann 'Assi' Hahn recalled sleeping with a loaded revolver under his pillow each night when the building 'came alive with sleek grey rats'!

and subsequently written-off in crash landings.

By this time other *Jagdgruppen* were slowly beginning to congregate along the Channel coast after their month's sojourn in the Homeland. Such was the leisurely nature of the build-up, however, that very little had been done in preparation for their arrival other than to allocate each of them some handy, open – and relatively flat – space in which to set up shop. At Desvres Hauptmann Kienitz's III./JG 3 thus found themselves operating from the local football pitches, and III./JG 54, under Hauptmann Ultsch, would return from a brief stay in Holland to take up residence at Guines-South, near Calais, on a sheep pasture so deeply rutted with animal tracks that take-offs and landings were at first regarded as more hazardous than the sorties flown in between.

Another *Jagdgruppe* had to harvest an entire wheatfield before they could commence operations from it. No such niceties for a *Luftflotte* 3 pilot who recalls being ordered after one early mission to land blind in a huge area of standing wheat some 1 1/2 metres high. Gingerly he did so, his prop scything a narrow swathe through the crop. When the stalks and the dust had settled the rest of his *Schwarm* followed exactly in his wheel tracks. It was impossible for them to take off again, so that evening the wheat was simply rolled flat, not cut. Next day the remainder of the *Gruppe* arrived and Beaumont-le-Roger – one of JG 2's major bases for the next four years – was ready for business!

Another early *Luftflotte* 3 arrival was I./JG 27. Returning from Bremen, they settled in at Plumetôt in Normandy, only to lose their *Kommandeur* almost immediately; Hauptmann Helmut Riegel being shot down by Hurricanes off Dover on 20 July. His keen interest in Germany's former colonies had prompted him to design the *Gruppe*'s now famous badge of the negro and tiger's head superimposed on a silhouette of Africa. It was ironic that within the year the *Gruppe* would be embarking on its finest hour over that very continent (see *Aircraft of the Aces 2*).

III./JG 52 lost their *Kommandeur* equally quickly – on 24 July, only 48 hours after arriving at Calais-Coquelles from Berlin, Hauptmann Wolf Dietrich von Houwald and two of his *Staffelkapitäne* were all killed in a disastrous clash with No 610 Sqn Spitfires over Kent. It took a week to name von Houwald's successor, but the two *Staffelkapitäne* were replaced immediately. One fell to the selfsame Spitfires of No 610 Sqn off Folkestone the very next day, whilst the other – Oberleutnant Günther Rall – would survive to become the third-highest scoring fighter pilot in history. But such was the effect of these, and other, early losses on the *Gruppe* that they were withdrawn back to Germany again before the month was out.

III./JG 26 had also been over Kent on 24 July immediately prior to III./JG 52's mauling at the hands of No 610 Sqn. They too had a new *Kommandeur*, as the previous incumbent, the same Major von Berg who had arrived from I./JG 51 under not the happiest of circumstances, had

The Bf 109E in the foreground (top) was assigned to Oberleutnant Günther Bode (*Adjutant* of I./JG 27), and it clearly shows the famous 'colonial' badge designed by *Kommandeur* Hauptmann Riegel long before the *Gruppe* saw service in Africa. Just visible behind the cockpit of 'Yellow 11' landing in the background is another wordplay emblem devised by Leutnant Ulrich Scherer, *Schwarmführer* in 3./JG 27, who was posted missing in the same action as Helmut Riegel. The German for scissors is '*Schere*', and the *Schwarm* badge of a pair of scissors plus the letter 'r' is clearly visible on 'Yellow 12' (above), brought down by a No 253 Sqn Hurricane over Kent on 30 August

proved to be a disappointing combat leader. His place had been taken early in June by the *Adjutant* of JG 27, Hauptmann Adolf Galland. And in this, JG 26's first sortie over England, Galland downed the Spitfire of Plt Off J L 'Johnny' Allen, DFC, an eight-kill ace of No 54 Sqn. He lost two of his own pilots, however, and later commented that this introduction to fighting the RAF over its home ground was a sobering experience.

And if Galland had arrived on the scene, could the redoubtable Mölders be far behind? Sure enough, Oberst Osterkamp was informed of his promotion to the position of *Jagdfliegerführer* 2. His place at the head of JG 51 was to be filled by Major Werner Mölders. 'Onkel Theo', who had retained a marked respect for the British from the earlier war – he always referred to them as the 'Lords' – offered some avuncular words of advice about not underestimating the opponents across the Channel, but to little avail.

Flying at the head of elements of I. and II./JG 51 on his first mission over England on 28 July, Mölders lost three of his fighters to No 74 Sqn

Snugly ensconced in the bottom half of a padded ex-RAF Irvin flying suit, Adolf Galland studies his dismantled *Emil*. The rigid posture of the two 'black men' would seem to indicate that the *Kommandeur* is none too pleased at what he sees. III./JG 26, Audembert, summer 1940

Werner Mölders (far right), now *Kommodore* of JG 51, in an altogether more relaxed mood. On the left, sporting the Knight's Cross, is Hauptmann Walter Oesau, *Kommandeur* of III./JG 51, whilst centre left in the leather greatcoat is ex-World War 1 ace, and newly promoted *Jafü* 2, 'Onkel Theo' Osterkamp

Below and right
Mölders in the ascendant – the *Kommodore's* aircraft (Wk-Nr 2804) displays 28 victory markings on 28 August 1940. Three days later and the 32nd is being painted on

Spitfires near Dover and had three more damaged. He was himself piloting one of the latter, which was raked from nose to tail by fire from Sqn Ldr 'Sailor' Malan, DFC, (6 kills at the time, and 34 by war's end). The wounded Mölders nursed his crippled Bf 109 back across the Channel for a crash landing at Wissant, and 'Onkel Theo' was permitted to lead his beloved JG 51 for a few days longer while the Luftwaffe's top-scoring ace recuperated.

Adolf Galland was awarded the Knight's Cross on 1 August for his

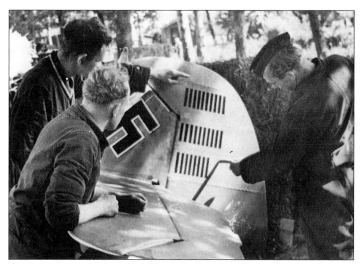

17 victories to date. That first week of August also saw RAF Bomber Command striking back hard, with II./JG 27 and II./JG 54 both suffering pilot fatalities and aircraft destroyed on their temporary Dutch bases.

But it was on 8 August that the first major *Jagdwaffe* losses were sustained, most of them aircraft of JG 27, which were escorting Ju 87s attacking a convoy off the Isle of Wight. One of the pilots downed, but subsequently recovered by the Luftwaffe's excellent air-sea rescue service, was Hauptmann Werner Andres, *Kommandeur* of II./JG 27. Despite the *Geschwader*'s best efforts, eight Stukas were destroyed and as many again damaged. This was but the first of an escalating series of multiple daily losses to be suffered by the hitherto seemingly invincible *Stukagruppen* which would ultimately result in their being withdrawn from the Battle altogether. The Bf 110 element of the escort on that 8 August raid was also roughly handled by the RAF. They too would suffer increasing losses as the Battle progressed, and end up requiring single-engined fighter protection themselves – a far cry from the all-conquering *Zerstörer* of Poland!

On both 11 and 12 August the *Jagdwaffe* reported 16 Bf 109s lost or

But if Mölders was on the way up, Hans-Jürgen von Cramon-Taubadel, *Kommodore* of JG 53, was on the way out. Having aroused Göring's ire by marrying into a family whose Aryan credentials were not quite 100 per cent, von Cramon was the only one of the 'Old Guard' *Kommodoren* not to receive the Knight's Cross, whilst his unit was collectively 'punished' by being ordered at the end of July to overpaint its proud 'Ace of Spades' insignia with a simple red band. The latter is clearly apparent on the Bf 109 of Hauptmann Günther von Maltzahn, *Kommandeur* of II./JG 53. The pilot standing in front of the aircraft is Gerhard Michalski, future 73-victory *Experte* and Oak Leaves recipient

And when Hauptmann Wolf-Dietrich Wilcke assumed command of III./JG 53 on 13 August upon the death of Harro Harder, he retaliated against Göring's 'political' order banning the 'Ace of Spades' by having the Swastika obliterated on all his *Gruppe*'s machines, as witness 'White 5' of 7./JG 53 seen here after being brought down over Kent on 6 September. Finally, on 20 November – the day of JG 53's 500th victory – the order was rescinded, the whole affair conveniently 'forgotten', and the 'Ace of Spades' reappeared to adorn the *Geschwader*'s fighters right up until war's end!

damaged from all causes. One of the casualties on the latter date was the *Gruppenkommandeur* of III./JG 53, Hauptmann Harro Harder, who disappeared after a dogfight east of the Isle of Wight during which he had claimed his 11th and 12th victories. His body was washed ashore near Dieppe a month later, but his memory was kept alive by his younger brother Jürgen, nearly all of whose later Bf 109s bore the name 'Harro' (see *Aircraft of the Aces 2* plates 47 and 48), before his own death in 1945 – the last of the three fighter-pilot Harder brothers to be killed on active service. On the credit side, the same 48 hours also saw the first kills for two future Knight's Cross *Experten* – II./JG 51's Alfred Rauch on 11 August, and Erich Schmidt of III./JG 53, the latter scoring the first of his 18 Battle of Britain victories on the 12th.

When, after several delays, *'Adlertag'* was finally launched on 13 August, it got off to something of a shaky start. One final last-minute postponement due to bad weather was heeded by most units, but not by all. Events gathered pace as the day progressed, however, and at its close the Luftwaffe had flown nearly 500 individual bomber sorties covered by twice that number of escorting fighters.

Combat losses among the single-engined fighters were remarkably light, with only five pilots killed or missing. But the Bf 109's notoriously short range was highlighted by Hauptmann Karl Ebbinghausen's II./JG 26 who, having lingered too long on the far side of the Channel, lost seven fighters through ditching, with five more damaged in belly landings after just scraping back across the French coast.

It was the following four weeks, culminating on 15 September – since commemmorated in England as 'Battle of Britain Day' – which were to see the highest rate of attrition among the *Jagdgruppen*. In that period close on 400 Bf 109s were lost or damaged – the equivalent of more than three complete *Geschwader*! But at the same time the intensity of action which these

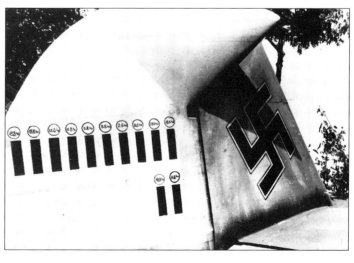

A *Schwarm* of 6./JG 27 high over the Channel during the Battle of Britain. The pilot taking this photograph, Oberleutnant Julius Neumann in 'Yellow 6', force-landed his stricken *Emil* on the Isle of Wight on 18 August – several published sources have credited his downfall to 19-kill ace Flt Sgt Jim 'Darkie' Hallowes of No 43 Sqn, who also downed a trio of Ju 87s in his Hurricane on the same day

Also over England on that 'Hardest Day', but with considerably more success, was Oberleutnant Gerhard Schöpfel of 9./JG 26. The last four kill markings on his rudder indicate the four No 501 Sqn Hurricanes he claimed near Canterbury on that date. Note too the new theatre marking – the upper segment of the rudder painted yellow

Scenes at III./JG 26's Caffiers base, August 1940. Gerhard Schöpfel's 'Yellow 1' in its camouflaged dispersal, 9.*Staffel's 'Höllenhund'* ('Hound from Hell') badge being prominently displayed both in red under the cockpit of the Bf 109 and in white on the door of the Mercedes-Benz 340

Constructing yet another sandbag blast pen similar to that protecting Schöpfel's machine

Groundcrew uncrate a replacement DB 601 newly arrived from Germany prior to carrying out an engine change

JG 26's first three Knight's Cross winners – left to right Schöpfel, Galland and Müncheberg

figures represent allowed the established *Experten* to continue adding to their scores, Galland, Müncheberg and Schöpfel each claimed victories the day after *'Adlertag'*, with Galland downing another three twenty-four hours later.

The second half of August also provided opportunities for newcomers to embark upon their climb to acedom, beginning with II./JG 27's Otto Schultz on the 15th and Karl 'Charly' Willius of III./JG 51 three days later. On 24 August a long-haired young Berliner, whose Bohemian big-city manners and

Hauptmann Horst 'Jakob' Tietzen, 7-victory *Condor Legion* ace, who commanded 5./JG 51 from the outbreak of war until his death on 18 August

On 22 August Major Adolf Galland was appointed *Kommodore* of JG 26. Here (left), he describes a recent combat to his attentive crew chief from the cockpit of an *Emil* bearing regulation *Geschwaderkommodore* markings plus his own personal *Mickey Mouse* insignia. Once on the ground, however, those other Galland 'trademarks' appear – the battered peak cap and omnipresent cigar!

irresponsible attitude to authority did not exactly endear him to his superiors in I.(J)/LG 2 and II./JG 52 during his time on the Channel coast, claimed his first – a Spitfire. It was not until after his posting to I./JG 27 early in 1941, and that unit's subsequent transfer to Africa, that Hans-

Another star was rising fast on the Channel front. Having gained the Knight's Cross for 20 victories on 27 August, Oberleutnant Helmut Wick of JG 2 was featured on the front page of a Berlin weekly magazine the following month – by which time his score was already past the 22 mark depicted in this propaganda shot

Oberleutnant Franz von Werra, *Gruppen-Adjutant* of II./JG 3, clambers cheerfully aboard his *Emil* at Samer's wooded dispersal . . .

. . . but it was no doubt a far more serious von Werra who was forced down by Australian ace Flt Lt Pat Hughes (17 kills – see *Aircraft of the Aces 12*) of No 234 Sqn over Kent on 5 September. Modellers should note that the scoreboard on the starboard side of the tailfin was slightly lower, and all eight aerial kills were grouped together, as there was no Werk-Nummer on that side

Joachim Marseille's true qualities would be recognised (see *Aircraft of the Aces 2*).

There was a whole clutch of new Knight's Cross recipients in August, including the first posthumous example when Hauptmann Horst Tietzen, *Staffelkapitän* of 5./JG 51, was honoured with the award two days after being reported missing over the Thames estuary (possibly the victim of No 85 Sqn's 11-kill Hurricane ace, Sqn Ldr Peter Townsend).

Although individual and collective scores continued to mount – Gerhard Schöpfel had claimed four No 501 Sqn Hurricanes in the space of two minutes on 18 August (the *Jagdflieger* later described the moments prior to the combat in the following terms; 'Suddenly I noticed a *Staffel* of Hurricanes underneath me. They were using the English tactics of the period, flying in close formation of threes, climbing in a wide spiral'), Günther Lützow a brace of Defiants on 24 August and Helmut Wick his nineteenth and twentieth twenty-four hours later (the day JG 2 scored their 250th victory of the war) – the Luftwaffe's latest offensive was not producing the hoped-for results. Part of Göring's answer was to begin replacing those 'Old Guard' *Kommodore* still remaining at the head of some *Jagdgeschwader* with younger pilots of proven combat ability. The end of August thus saw Adolf Galland and Hannes Trautloft in command of JGs 26 and 54 respectively.

Having entrusted these 'Young Turks' with improving his fighters' performance, the *Reichsmarschall* promptly tied their hands by ordering a change of tactics. The *Freie Jagd* type of mission, ranging far and wide ahead to clear the bombers' path, was out. Henceforth, the Bf 109s were to fly close-formation escort duty. 1 September, for example, found elements from three

Jagdgeschwader protecting a force of just 18 He 111s despatched against Tilbury docks.

Despite these constraints 'firsts' were still being scored. Future 133-victory ace Alfred Grislawski of JG 52 and JG 53's Werner Stumpf both achieved theirs during the Tilbury raid. Three days later Unteroffizier

While the vast bulk of one-way Channel traffic in the summer of 1940 was provided by the Luftwaffe, the occasional RAF fighter also 'failed to return' from the other side. One such was the Spitfire of No 603 Sqn's Plt Off J L Caister, who reportedly pursued a gaggle of Bf 109s to France on 6 September, only to be forced down by Hauptmann Hubertus von Bonin, *Kommandeur* of I./JG 54. Here, the Spitfire, propeller blades bent from its wheels-up landing, is seen alongside a partially stripped *Emil* at I./JG 54's Campagne-les-Guines dispersal

The British fighter is examined with interest by the *Gruppe*'s pilots before groundcrewmen give it a coat of overall light *(hellblau?)* paint. The ultimate fate of Spitfire XT-D, serial X4260, is unknown

Hubertus von Bonin's Bf 109E displays yet another variant of the *Mickey Mouse* theme, this one also dating back to Spain when it was the badge of the *Condor Legion*'s 3./J 88. Note too the white outline-only *Gruppenkommandeur* chevrons on the heavily mottled fuselage

Two September Knight's Cross winners – Hauptmann Rolf Pingel, *Gruppenkommandeur* of I./JG 26, received the award on the 14th . . .

. . . while Oberleutnant Hans 'Assi' Hahn, *Staffelkapitän* of 4./JG 2, gained his ten days later

Kurt Bühligen of JG 2, who would remain with the same *Geschwader* throughout the war and rise to become its tenth and final *Kommodore*, claimed the first of his 112 western victories.

But there were losses too. On 5 September – when Hauptmann Otto Bertram of III./JG 2 claimed his third double in four days – the *Gruppen-Adjutant* of II./JG 3 was forced down over Kent. The eight aerial victories indicated on the latter's tailfin may not have been unique, but his subsequent escape from captivity in Canada and return to Germany to fly and fight again certainly was, for Oberleutnant Franz von Werra was the 'One that got away'. No such luck next day for Hauptmann Joachim Schlichting, *Kommandeur* of III./JG 27, who was one of four JG 27 pilots shot down and captured. He would be awarded the Knight's Cross in December in recognition of his 'excellent performance in protecting the bomber formations he escorted with no thought for his own personal success' – he had achieved just three kills.

The remaining weeks of September continued to exact a steady toll of the *Jagdwaffe*'s men and machines, including 'Battle of Britain Day' when

By this time the other Channel front Hahn – Hans von – was *Gruppenkommandeur* of I./JG 3 at Colombert. His earlier cockerel's head badge (see photo on page 33) has now been moved aft to make way for the *Gruppe's* 'Tatzelwurm' (Dragon) emblem on the cowling

These I./JG 3 *Emils* at Colombert in September all display the square style of numeral favoured by the *Gruppe* . . .

. . . as too does 2.*Staffel*'s 'Black 6', which returned somewhat the worse for wear from operations over southern England

But as Unteroffizier Keller walks disconsolately away from his battered Bf 109 an additional refinement is revealed – white wingtip markings

One which didn't get back was Bf 109E-3 'White 4' (Wk-Nr 1190) of 4./JG 26, force-landed by Unteroffizier Horst Perez near Eastbourne on 30 September. It should be noted that the proud Tommy standing at attention in front of the machine is hiding not just the number '4' but also 4.*Staffel*'s 'Tiger's head' badge. This *Emil* was subsequently shipped to Canada and the United States for propaganda purposes, before being returned to the UK some 20 years later! It currently resides in Dorset

By mid-October another three victories had been added to the tail of Wilhelm Balthasar's Wk-Nr 1559. Having been seriously wounded on 4 September over Canterbury by a Spitfire from No 222 Sqn, it would take him a full year to add 17 kills to the 23 aerial victories he had scored over France in just six weeks. As *Kommodore* of JG 2 he would receive the Oak Leaves for his 40th on 2 July 1941, only to be killed in action 24 hours later

On 19 October the *Staffelkapitän* of 6./JG 51, Oberleutnant Josef Priller, received the Knight's Cross for 20 victories, each one carefully recorded in straight lines (parallel to the ground rather than the axis of the aircraft!) right across the tailfin Swastika of his 'Yellow 1'!

Left **But Perez was no ace. The five victory bars on Wk-Nr 1190 (two Dutch, one French and two British) were left behind by its previous 'owner', Hauptmann Karl Ebbighausen, *Staffelkapitän* of 4./JG 26, when he was promoted to the command of II.*Gruppe*. Ebbighausen must have scored two more kills on his new mount, for his final tally was standing at seven when he was shot down by a No 266 Sqn Spitfire near Deal on 16 August**

19 Bf 109s failed to return. But the 'Old Firm' of Mölders and Galland was still going strong. They received the Oak Leaves to their Knight's Crosses just four days apart, on 21 and 25 September respectively, for each scoring 40 victories. Both were also given a few days leave to celebrate. While Galland was away, the *Gruppenkommandeur* of I./JG 26, Hauptmann Rolf Pingel, took over as acting *Kommodore* only to fall victim to a No 238 Sqn Hurricane over the Channel on 28 September.

Oberleutnant Helmut Wick (left) illustrates a steep bank for the benefit of *Gruppenkommandeur* Major Hennig Strümpell

Having successfully ditched, he was rescued some hours later by an ASR aircraft. On hearing the news, Galland was unsympathetic; 'I leave him alone for one day to go hunting in East Prussia, and straightaway old Pingel gets himself shot down!'

On 30 September the *Jagdgruppen* sustained their heaviest casualties of the entire Battle with no fewer than 28 Bf 109s lost. Forty-eight hours later Göring rubbed salt into the wound by ordering that a third of all his Channel-based *Jagdgeschwader* strength be converted into fighter-bombers for tip-and-run *Jabo* sorties.

While Mölders and Galland had been vying with each other over the Straits of Dover and south-eastern England, further west along the Channel *Luftflotte* 3's brightest star, one Helmut Wick, was climbing hard on their heels. Already wearing the Knight's Cross, and now risen from *Staffelkapitän* of 3./JG 2 to *Kommandeur* of I. *Gruppe*, Hauptmann Wick's most successful day of the Battle was 5 October when he downed a trio of Hurricanes (of No 607 Sqn) off the Isle of Wight early in the afternoon and then claimed another two kills (probably from No 238 Sqn) during a second sortie. This brought his total to 42, earning him the Oak Leaves and promotion to Major.

Nevertheless, it was Mölders who was selected to receive the first three Bf 109F-0 pre-production machines for service evaluation at this juncture of the Battle. He flew his first sortie in the new model on 9 October, and its superiority over the Emil in terms of performance, if not fire-power, was immediately apparent.

In more restrained mood, the now Hauptmann Wick (right) is pictured here with Major Wolfgang Schellmann, *Geschwader-kommodore* JG 2

This fact was forcibly brought home to one of his *Stabskette* just over a fortnight later. Flying Mölder's old Bf 109E, Hauptmann Hans Asmus was unable to keep up with the faster *Friedrichs* of his companions after they had been bounced by Hurricanes of No 501 Sqn, and he was shot down to spend the rest of the war in captivity.

By this time the Battle was winding down rapidly. Operation *Sealion*, the planned invasion of

With the Battle winding down, it was time to pick up the pieces. Many and varied were the examples of *Jagdwaffe* heraldry which littered England's southern counties, such as this 'Pink devil' of 'Short' Schumann's 5./JG 52 – the *'Rabatz'* or 'Troublemaker' *Staffel* – which never made it back to Calais-Peuplingues

Hauptmann Hans-Karl Mayer, *Gruppenkommandeur* of I./JG 53, posted missing over the Channel in an unarmed Bf 109E-7 on 17 October

When his two brothers were lost in action, Hauptmann Otto Bertram, *Kommandeur* of III./JG 2, was retired from operational flying to spend the rest of the war in various staff appointments and in command of training units

southern England, had been shelved on 12 October. Five days later Knight's Cross holder Hauptmann Hans-Karl Mayer, *Kommandeur* of I./JG 53, was lost in somewhat unusual circumstances. He was listed as missing on a test flight – indeed, he had taken off in an unarmed Bf 109E-7 replacement aircraft which had just been ferried in, but despite his also being minus a radio and dinghy, it appears Mayer in fact set off after his *Gruppe* which was in difficulties over the Channel. What happened next is uncertain (his loss was credited to Spitfires of No 603 Sqn), but his body was washed ashore on the Kent coast on 27 October.

The day after Mayer's body was found a Bf 110 nightfighter of III./NJG 1 crashed in Schleswig-Holstein, killing its crew. The pilot was Unteroffizier Karl Bertram, whose brother Hans, *Gruppen-Adjutant* of I./JG 27, had been downed over Sussex on 30 September. His family invoked the 'last surviving son' rule, and the third brother, Hauptmann Otto Bertram, ex-*Condor Legion* ace and now *Kommandeur* of III./JG 2, was retired from combat and awarded the Knight's Cross.

Despite the slackening of activity, the list of Knight's Cross winners – many soon-to-be-famous names among them – had continued to lengthen during October and into November. But the triumvirate of Mölders, Galland and Wick were still way ahead of all others. Mölders had claimed his 50th victory on 22 October, with Galland following suit nine days later. By 28 November they had added just four and two more kills to their respective scores, and for a brief few days the famous pair were to be eclipsed.

In mid-November Stabsfeldwebel Willinger had scored JG 2's 500th victory of the war – 54 of that total had been achieved by the Richthofen *Geschwader*'s new *Kommodore*, for on 20 October Major Wick had reached the pinnacle of his meteoric rise. He had been appointed to the head of arguably the most famous fighter unit in the Luftwaffe. It was an inspired choice, for the 25-year-old Wick was not just a natural combat pilot, but also a gifted leader. He displayed the same sort of care and con-

As *Kapitän* of 1./JG 2, 'Otsch' Bertram had introduced the *Staffel*'s 'Bonzo dog' emblem seen here on the cowling of his 'White 1', which he force-landed near Cambrai on 19 May after claiming his fourth kill at the height of the French campaign

By the end of October the cult of the 'fighter ace' had taken firm hold in the Homeland. This magazine page is devoted to eight of the early Knight's Cross winners and is headed 'Not one of them over 30 years of age'

A more informal gathering of Knight's Cross holders during a visit by Ernst Udet, Chief of Aircraft Procurement and Supply. From left, Balthasar, Oesau, Galland, Udet, Mölders and Pingel

cern for his men that had won Mölders the nickname 'Vati' ('Daddy'), but he combined with it the outspokenness of a Galland. The latter's response to Göring when asked during the Battle if there was anything he needed – 'A squadron of Spitfires, Herr Reichsmarschall!' – is part of Luftwaffe history. Less well known, but equally revealing, was Wick's earlier reaction as a lowly *Kapitän* when his *Staffel* was being inspected by Generalfeldmarschall Hugo Sperrle, GOC *Luftflotte* 3. Sperrle commented, as Generals are wont to do, that the groundcrews could be a little less scruffy, only to be brusquely told that 'these men are working day and night to keep our fighters in the air and have better things to do than to get their hair cut!'

But Wick's term of command was to be short-lived. He had already claimed one victory over the Isle of Wight in the early afternoon of 28 November before, refuelled and rearmed, he led his *Stabsschwarm* back to his favourite hunting grounds south of the Solent. Sure enough, they spotted a squadron of Spitfires climbing to intercept them. The *Kommodore* and his wingman, Oberleutnant Rudolf Pflanz, dived to the attack and within moments Wick's 56th victim was going down in flames. It was to be his last. Recovering from the dive, Wick banked steeply, and for a split-second flashed across the nose of another Spitfire. Instinctively, its pilot, Flt Lt John 'Cocky' Dundas, DFC, of No 609 Sqn – himself a 16-victory Battle of Britain veteran – opened fire. The short burst must have mortally damaged the heavily mottled Messerschmitt, for Wick jettisoned his canopy and baled out. The solitary parachute drifting down towards the sea to the

Unlike many other *Jagdflieger*, Helmut Wick retained the same aircraft through most of the latter part of his brief, but illustrious, career. Here his E-4 (Wk-Nr 5344), seen on the vast expanse of flattened wheat that was Beaumont-le-Roger in the high summer of 1940, bears the 'Yellow 2' of his time as *Staffelkapitän* of 3./JG 2. Note the *Staffel* badge on the cowling, the *Geschwader* badge beneath the windscreen, the unusual presentation of the fuselage cross and the – unfortunately indistinct – number of kill bars on the rudder

Following Wick's promotion to *Kommandeur* of I./JG 2 on 7 September, the 'Yellow 2' has now given way to *Gruppen-kommandeur's* chevrons. Wk-Nr 5344 has also acquired a yellow nose and spinner, windscreen armour and a total of 32 victory markings

Still at Beaumont-le-Roger, Wick's E-4 sports another row of 10 victory bars, thus bringing his total to the 42 that won him the Oak Leaves on 6 October, plus promotion to *Geschwaderkommodore* of JG 2 exactly two weeks later. Otherwise the markings remain the same, but the new whitewall tailwheel tyre adds a nice touch!

south-west of the Needles would be the last anybody ever saw of the Luftwaffe's leading ace, for despite intensive air and sea searches no trace of Wick was ever found. Dundas shared a similar fate, downed seconds later off Bournemouth by 'Rudi' Pflanz.

The loss of Wick effectively wrote *finis* to the Battle. The worsening weather in the first week of December turned most of the *Jagdwaffe*'s grass fields along the coastal strip into quagmires of mud, and many *Gruppen* were retired further inland. During the course of the month they started withdrawing to Germany for the winter to rest and refit – which was an

This close-up of Wk-Nr 5344's tail shows Wick's score – 54 – as it stood on the eve of his being posted missing. It also gives a very good impression of the densely-mottled camouflage finish, although it is uncertain whether the peculiar rudder paintwork is deliberate or some chemical reaction of the yellow to the coat beneath it. By this time the *Gruppen-kommandeur*'s chevrons have in their turn been replaced by a regulation set of *Geschwader-kommodore* tactical markings as depicted in Iain Wyllie's cover painting for this book

Two final ironies surround Wicks' loss. Moments after he had taken off on his final flight an order was received at *Geschwader* HQ prohibiting him from all further combat flying. He was now considered too valuable to risk, and henceforth was to use his remarkable skills in training new pilots. Also, he once again adorned the cover of Berlin's best-selling weekly. Here he is on the far right of the picture captioned 'The Reichsmarschall visits the *Jagdgeschwader Richthofen*', and the date of Issue No 48, top left . . . 28 November 1940!

Wick may have gone, but Galland and Mölders continued to match each other kill for kill. In December the tail of Galland's E-4/N (Wk-Nr 5819) at Audembert displayed 57 . . .

open invitation for the RAF to begin its 'lean forward' into France.

The 'lean' was made official on 10 January 1941 with the mounting of Circus No 1, a raid on France by six Blenheims covered by no fewer than eleven fighter squadrons. The wheel of cross-Channel air warfare had turned full circle as the RAF now began its fight back. And although these

85

early 'Circuses' continued to provide opportunities for the pilots of the Luftwaffe's Bf 109Es to add to their scores – future JG 3 Knight's Cross recipients Hans von Hahn and Georg Michalek both claimed kills on 10 January, and Walter Oesau's 40th achieved on 5 February against Circus No 3 to St Omer would win him his Oak Leaves – the days of the *Emil* in the west were numbered.

The Bf 109E would continue to soldier on with some units along the Channel until well into the summer, and longer with the new JG 1 in the coastal regions of Holland and northern Germany. It would even go on to regain some of its earlier glory over the Balkans and in the opening months of the North African and Russian campaigns. But in the west it was gradually being supplanted as the *Jagdgruppen* returned from their winter breaks in the Homeland either already re-equipped with, or soon to begin conversion to, the Bf 109F. By mid-1941 the *Emil* on the Channel front was more likely to be the victim rather than the victor as the RAF introduced the new Spitfire Mk V, although it was anti-aircraft fire from an RN destroyer which brought down Hauptmann Werner Machold, *Staffelkapitän* of 7./JG 2 and 32-kill ace from the heady days of summer 1940, during a low-level *Jabo* attack on a convoy off Portland on 9 June.

. . . while the *Emil* of Mölders, who is seen here wearing the Oak Leaves and chatting to Walter Oesau (right), was soon to be adorned with the 60th kill of its illustrious pilot

Göring's autumn visits to the Channel front were eclipsed by no less a personage than Adolf Hitler himself, who made a Christmas tour of selected Luftwaffe bases. Here he partakes of a festive meal in JG 3's mess with *Geschwaderkommodore* Major Günther Lützow sitting on his left – but it is the expression on the face of the orderly immediately behind the *Führer* that repays a second look!

The winter lull. Standing in the snow in front of Gerhard Schöpfel's Bf 109 in January 1941 is JG 26's Technical Officer Oberleutnant Walter Horten. A stern critic of the way the battle had been run by the High Command, Horten would soon leave the *Geschwader* to rejoin his brother Reimar in researching their revolutionary flying-wing designs

The *Emils* were retiring too. Galland's Wk-Nr 5819, now with 60 victory markings, is pictured at Brest in April 1941, with the *Kommodore*'s brand-new Bf 109F-0 just visible in the background

With 82 kills on her rudder and Galland's famous *Mickey Mouse* still beneath the cockpit – but with the *Kommodore*'s markings replaced by *Gruppenkommandeur*'s chevrons – 5819 served out her time with JG 26's *Ergänzungsgruppe* (Training and Replacement Wing) at Cazaux on the French Biscay coast

But it was the loss of Oberfeldwebel Robert Menge – highest scorer of the Norwegian campaign and more recently Adolf Galland's wingman in the *Stabsschwarm* JG 26 now with 18 kills to his credit – which most conclusively closes the chapter on the early Bf 109 *Experten*. He was shot down and killed by Sqn Ldr Jamie Rankin (22 kills) of No 92 Sqn while taking off from Marquise in response to Circus No 12 on 14 June, just one week prior to the invasion of the Soviet Union.

And of those aces who had shone so brightly, yet so briefly, during the early campaigns? Gentzen of Poland, Wick and now Menge were already gone. Balthasar, the highest scorer in France, and Mölders were soon to follow. Only two would survive the war – Schumacher of German Bight fame from behind a desk, and Adolf Galland in the cockpit of that other masterpiece from the Messerschmitt stable, the Me 262 jet fighter.

But the man himself soldiered on – from the open cockpit of a Henschel Hs 123 ground-assault biplane in Poland to the Me 262 jet fighter in the final cataclysmic days of the *Reich*, Adolf Galland was the archetypal Luftwaffe combat leader of World War 2

THE APPENDICES

Bf 109E Knight's Cross Recipients 29/5/40 - 22/6/41

	Unit at Time of Award	Date of Award	Victories at Time of Award	Total No WWII Victories	(Plus Spain)	Lost (KiA, MiA or PoW)
Mölders, *Hptm* Werner	JG 53	29/5/40	20	101	(14)	22/11/41
Balthasar, *Hptm* Wilhelm	JG 27	14/6/40	23	40	(7)	3/7/41
Schumacher, *Oberstlt* Carl	JG 1	21/7/40	2	2	-	-
Galland, *Maj* Adolf	JG 26	1/8/40	17	104	-	-
Tietzen, *Hptm* Horst	JG 51	20/8/40(+)	20	20	(7)	18/8/40
Oesau, *Hptm* Walter	JG 51	20/8/40	20	117	(8)	11/5/44
von Bülow-Bothkamp, *Oberstlt* Harry	JG 2	22/8/40	-	-	-	-
Ibel, *Oberst* Max	JG 27	22/8/40	-	-	-	-
Osterkamp, *Genmaj.* Theo	Jafü 2	22/8/40	6 *	6	-	-
Wick, *Oblt* Helmut	JG 2	27/8/40	20	56	-	28/11/40
Mayer, *Hptm* Hans-Karl	JG 53	3/9/40	20	31	(8)	17/10/40
Machold, *Obfw* Werner	JG 2	5/9/40	21	32	-	6/6/41
Schöpfel, *Hptm* Gerhard	JG 26	11/9/40	20	40	-	-
Ihlefeld, *Oblt* Herbert	LG 2	13/9/40	21	123	(7)	-
Müncheberg, *Oblt* Joachim	JG 26	14/9/40	20	135	-	23/3/43
Pingel, *Hptm* Rolf	JG 26	14/9/40	15	22	(4)	10/7/41
Joppien, *Oblt* Hermann-Friedrich	JG 51	16/9/40	21	70	-	25/8/41
Lützow, *Hptm* Günther	JG 3	18/9/40	15	103	(5)	24/4/45
Schellmann, *Maj* Wolfgang	JG 2	18/9/40	10	14	(12)	22/6/41
Hahn, *Oblt* Hans	JG 2	24/9/40	20	108	-	21/2/43
Lippert, *Hptm* Wolfgang	JG 27	24/9/40	12	25	(4)	3/12/41
Sprick, *Ltn* Gustav	JG 26	1/10/40	20	31	-	28/6/41
Priller, *Oblt* Josef	JG 51	19/10/40	20	101	-	-
Hrabak, *Hptm* Dietrich	JG 54	21/10/40	16	125	-	-
Bretnütz, *Hptm* Otto	JG 53	22/10/40	20	35	(2)	27/6/41
Philipp, *Oblt* Hans	JG 54	22/10/40	20	206	-	8/10/43
Bertram, *Hptm* Otto	JG 2	28/10/40	13	13	(8)	-
Ebeling, *Oblt* Heinz	JG 26	5/11/40	18	18	-	5/11/40
Lignitz, *Oblt* Arnold	JG 54	5/11/40	19	25	-	30/9/41
Schnell, *Ltn* Siegfried	JG 2	9/11/40	20	93	-	25/2/44
Adolph, *Hptm* Walter	JG 26	13/11/40	15	28	(1)	18/9/41
Krahl, *Hptm* Karl-Heinz	JG 2	13/11/40	15	24	-	14/4/42
Hintze, *Oblt* Otto	Erp.Gr.210	24/11/40	1	1	-	29/10/40
Schlichting, *Hptm* Joachim	JG 27	14/12/40	3	3	(5)	6/9/40
von Werra, *Oblt* Franz	JG 3	14/12/40	8	21	-	25/10/41
von Maltzahn, *Maj* Günther Freiherr	JG 53	30/12/40	13	68	-	-
Bob, *Oblt* Hans-Ekkehard	JG 54	7/3/41	19	59	-	-
Rudorffer, *Ltn* Erich	JG 2	1/5/41	19	222	-	-
Homuth, *Oblt* Gerhard	JG 27	14/6/41	22	63	-	3/8/43
Rödel, *Oblt* Gustav	JG 27	22/6/41	20	98	-	-

(+) Posthumous

* Plus 32 in World War 1

The list on page 88 clearly illustrates the two types of early Knight's Cross recipients – the 'Old Guard' (Schumacher, Osterkamp *et al*) who received the award in recognition of their qualities of leadership, and the 'Young Bloods' (led by Mölders, Balthasar and Galland) who were honoured for their prowess in combat. At this stage of the war a total of 20 victories assured a fighter pilot of his Knight's Cross, although anomalies and special cases were already appearing. The 20-kill benchmark was gradually increased as the war progressed, and by mid-1944 some members of JG 52 in the east had downed 100-125 enemy aircraft before the award was conferred.

Six of the pilots listed would double their

score to 40+ before June 1941 and receive the Oak Leaves – Mölders (21/9/40), Galland (25/9/40), Wick (6/10/40), Oesau (6/2/41), Joppien (23/4/41) and Müncheberg (7/5/41).

On 21/6/41, with 69 kills, Adolf Galland became the first member of the entire Wehrmacht to win the Swords, beating Mölders by just 24 hours. The following month, on 16/7/41, Werner Mölders, now flying on the eastern front, was to regain premier place by achieving the same distinction with the Diamonds for being the first fighter pilot in the world to top the 100 mark. Galland would still be six short of his century in the west when he received the Diamonds on 28/1/42.

COLOUR PLATES

1
Bf 109E-3 'Black Chevron and Bars' of Oberstleutnant Carl Schumacher, *Geschwaderkommodore* JG 1, Jever, Spring 1940

Although not an ace in the strictest sense, Schumacher's pivotal role in early Bf 109 operations in north Germany warrants the inclusion of one of the aircraft he flew. This pristine *Emil* bears perfectly standard camouflage and regulation *Kommodore's* tactical markings of the period. Note, however, that although the early style *Stab* JG 1 badge is carried below the windscreen, there is no indication of Schumacher's two (and only) kills to date – his No 37 Sqn Wellington IA of 18 December 1939 and the No 107 Sqn Blenheim IV claimed nine days later.

2
Bf 109E-4 (Wk-Nr 1486) 'White 1' of Hauptmann Wilhelm Balthasar, *Staffelkapitän* of 1./JG 1, Monchy-Breton, May 1940

Despite wearing a similar finish to the machine above, the I./JG 1 of 1939-40 bore no relationship to Schumacher's *Stab* JG 1. It was instead a hitherto autonomous East Prussian *Gruppe* which, after the Battle of France, would be redesignated III./JG 27 (witness the *Gruppe* badge beneath the cockpit and the unit's near unique practice of displaying its individual numerals on the engine cowling). Balthasar's aircraft is further identified by the *Staffelkapitän's* metal pennant on the aerial mast and the 11 victory bars on the tailfin, the last two being Spitfires (probably of No 19 Sqn) over Calais on 26 May.

3
Bf 109E-4 (Wk-Nr 5344) 'Black Double Chevron' of Hauptmann Helmut Wick, *Gruppenkommandeur* of I./JG 2 'Richthofen', Beaumont-le-Roger, October 1940

Depicted midway in its evolution from 'Yellow 2' to full

Kommodore's markings (see photos on pages 84/85 and cover), it is hard to believe that Wk-Nr 5344 too must have looked very similar to the two previous profiles before it received its coat of very close dapple overall. Note also the 'toning down' of the fuselage cross by reducing the white areas, and the pale yellow cowling (thin yellow wash over white). Certain inconsistencies in the presentation and grouping of the victory bars point to 5344's having had a number of replacement rudders during its career. The 'Richthofen' *Geschwader* badge is carried beneath the windscreen, while that on the cowling (long thought to be Wick's personal emblem) is the insignia of 3./JG 2, designed some time earlier by a *Staffel* member who chose the colours blue and yellow in honour of the then *Kapitän* Hennig Strümpell's Swedish ancestry.

4
Bf 109E 'Chevron-Triangle' of Major Dr Erich Mix, *Gruppenkommandeur* III./JG 2 'Richthofen, France, May 1940

This *Emil* offers an example of the 'outline only' style of rank and *Gruppe* markings to be seen on some Bf 109s in the early summer of 1940. Dr Mix's three World War 1 victories did not qualify him for acedom in that particular conflict, so he finished the job in the second by adding thirteen more, the first two being marked here on the rudder of the machine he force-landed behind the French lines near Roye on 21 May. After subsequent service as *Kommodore* of JG 1 (1942-43), he became *Jafü* Bretagne (Fighter Leader Britanny).

5
Bf 109E-4 'White 1' of Oberleutnant Werner Machold, *Staffelkapitän* 7./JG 2 'Richthofen', Le Havre, September 1940

Machold's machine displays a certain amount of overspraying, not to say downright wear and tear, as the Battle of Britain

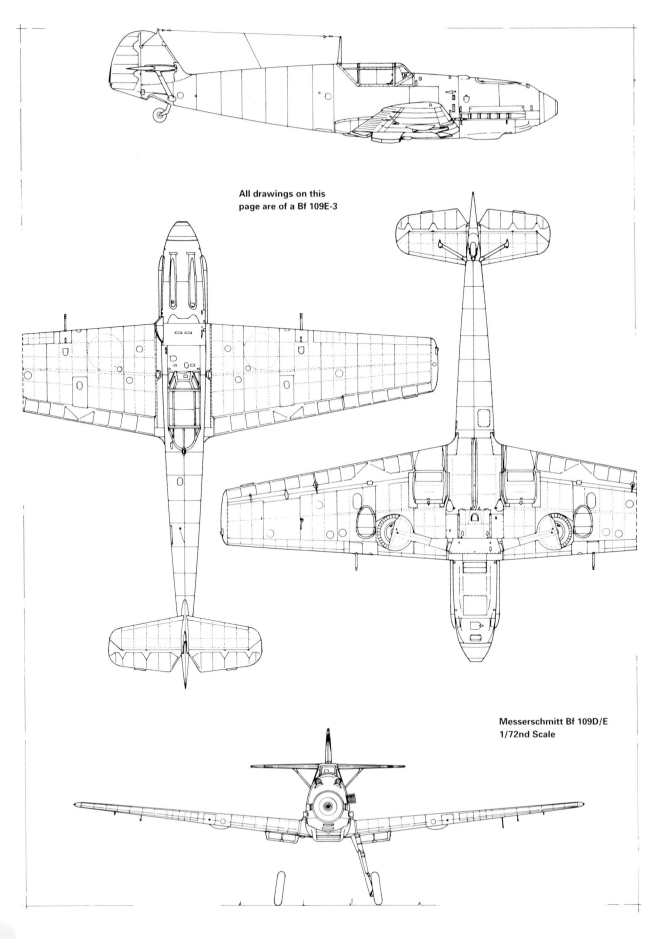

All drawings on this
page are of a Bf 109E-3

Messerschmitt Bf 109D/E
1/72nd Scale

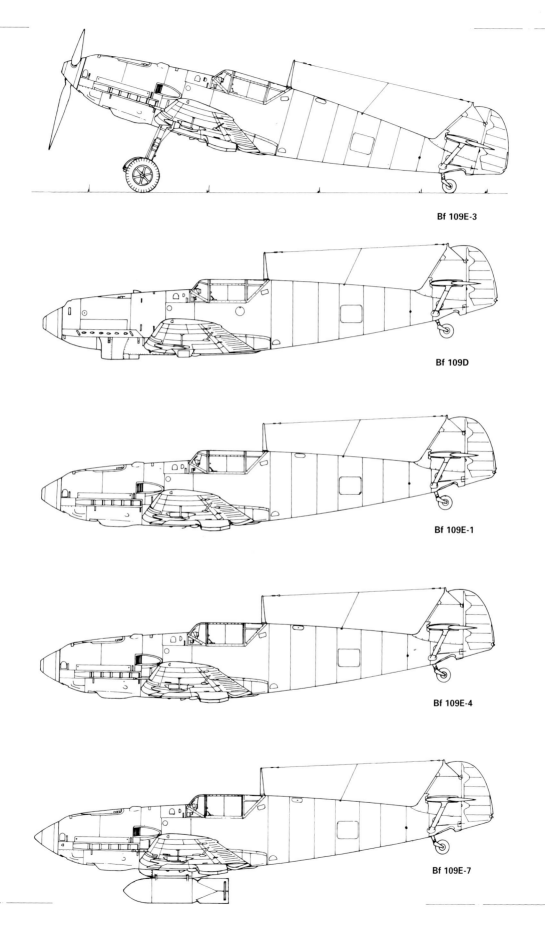

Bf 109E-3

Bf 109D

Bf 109E-1

Bf 109E-4

Bf 109E-7

nears its end. The 26 victory markings on the rudder dates it as late September. Note the more usual 'solid' numeral and *Gruppe* wavy bar (compared to the machine above), and also *Geschwader* and *Staffel* badges, the latter – a 'Thumb pressing a top hat' – being a co-design of Leutnant Schmidt and Oberfeldwebel Klee. Machold (pictured on the back cover wearing the Knight's Cross) claimed six more kills before force-landing in Dorset after damage sustained attacking a Channel convoy on 9 June 1941.

6

Bf 109E-4 (Wk-Nr 1559) 'Green 1' of Hauptmann Wilhelm Balthasar, *Gruppenkommandeur* III./JG 3, Desvres, August 1940

When promoted from *Kapitän* of 7./JG 27 (the ex-1./JG 1, see profile 2) to *Gruppenkommandeur* of III./JG 3 late in August, Balthasar took with him the *Emil* he had last been flying in his old *Staffel*, and on which he had gained many of his French campaign victories. This explains the odd duplication of markings, for he initially retained the III./JG 27 badge forward of the windscreen and the 'White 1' carried on the cowling. Over the latter he superimposed III./JG 3's 'Battle axe' badge, and also added a green tip to the spinner (green being the colour for *Stab* aircraft) plus, more unusually, opted for a green '1' – and III.*Gruppe* vertical bar – rather than for regulation *Kommandeur*'s chevrons.

7

Bf 109E-4 (Wk-Nr 1480) 'Black Chevron' of Oberleutnant Franz von Werra, *Gruppen-Adjutant* II./JG 3, Samer, August 1940

Von Werra's aircraft carries the other standard, but fractionally less common, Battle of Britain tactical recognition markings of white cowling and rudder, together with regulation *Adjutant*'s chevron, III.*Gruppe* badge and horizontal bar. The only sign of individuality is provided by the 13 kill symbols (8 aerial victories, 5 destroyed on the ground) displayed on both sides of the tail-fin (see photo on page 76). After his epic escape from Canada, and return to Germany via the USA, von Werra resumed combat flying as *Gruppenkommandeur* of I./JG 53 on the eastern front, where he achieved a further 13 victories in just three weeks. This *Gruppe* was then withdrawn for re-equipment with Bf 109Fs, and it was while flying a *Friedrich* that von Werra was killed after suffering engine failure off the Dutch coast on 25 October 1941.

8

Bf 109E-4 'Black Chevron and Triangle' of Hauptmann Hans von Hahn, *Gruppenkommandeur* I./JG 3, Colombert, August 1940

Compared to the previous machine, 'Vadder' von Hahn's E-4 may almost be described as 'exuberant', with its yellow cowling and rudder, multi-coloured spinner, I.*Gruppe* 'Tatzelwurm' ('Dragon') emblem in *Stab* green and the pilots personal 'cockerel' badge. Most interesting, however, is the treatment of the *Gruppenkommandeur*'s insignia, von Hahn choosing to enlarge the small inner triangle and present it as a separate marking aft of the main chevron. Von Hahn oversaw I./JG 3's redesignation into II./JG 1 early in 1942, before undertaking a series of staff appointments. He ended the war with 34 victories as *Jafü* Oberitalien (Fighter Leader Upper Italy).

9

Bf 109E-4 'Black Chevron-Triangle and Bar' of Hauptmann Hannes Trautloft, *Gruppenkommandeur* I./JG 20, Bönninghardt, March 1940

Displaying a transitional fuselage cross (ie, of the smaller pre-war size but in the new proportions with wider borders) and a tail Swastika still centered on the rudder hinge line, Trautloft's *Emil* features two other items of interest – the new 'Axe of the Lower-Rhine' *Gruppe* badge adopted upon the move from the Berlin area to Bönningshardt, south-west of Wesel, early in 1940, and the *Kommandeur*'s chevron-triangle to which Trautloft has added a vertical bar. This unusual – arguably unique – combination was long regarded as the markings used to signfy a *Geschwaderkommodore*. I./JG 20 was subsequently redesignated III./JG 51, but Trautloft's name is more closely linked with JG 54, which he led from 1940 to 1943.

10

Bf 109E-4/N (Wk-Nr 5819) 'Black Chevron and Bars' of Oberstleutnant Adolf Galland, *Geschwaderkommodore* JG 26 'Schlageter', Audembert, December 1940

Undoubtedly one of the best known *Emils* of them all, Galland's famous E-4/N comes complete with *Kommodore* markings, 57 victory bars on the rudder and the familiar black-and-white *Mickey Mouse* personal emblem. But the writing was on the wall for the *Emil* – just three more kills and it would be sharing its Brest dispersal with the *Kommodore*'s new Bf 109F-0. One minor point of interest – that was not a telescopic sight projecting through the windscreen, but a straightforward telescope which enabled Galland to identify between friend and foe at a greater range . . . it's that extra edge which makes all the difference!

11

Bf 109E 'Red 16' of Oberleutnant Fritz Losigkeit, *Staffelkapitän* of 2./JG 26 'Schlageter', Bönninghardt, March 1940

A standard *hellblau* finish early Bf 109E immediatley prior to the campaign in the west, Losigkeit's machine displays both *Geschwader* and *Staffel* emblems. He would serve throughout the Battles of France and Britain before departing in May 1941 to take up an attaché's post at the German Embassy in Tokyo. Upon his return he would first command I./JG 1 in the west before transferring to JG 51 on the eastern front. He ended the war as *Kommodore* of JG 77 with a final tally of 68 victories.

12

Bf 109E-4 'Yellow 1' of Oberleutnant Gerhard Schöpfel, *Staffelkapitän* of 9./JG 26 'Schlageter', Caffiers, August 1940

Generally similar to Losigkeit's *Emil* immediately above, Schöpfel's aircraft is distinguished by the 'Höllenhund' ('Hound from Hell') 9.*Staffel* badge, yellow vertical III.*Gruppe* bar and *Staffel* trim (numeral and pennant). The passage of time from Battle of France to Battle of Britain is also indicated by the addition of new theatre recognition markings: yellow rudder segment and tail and wingtips. The last four of the twelve victory symbols shown record the four No 501 Sqn Hurricanes claimed by Schöpfel in a matter of minutes during the afternoon of 18 August. He too would survive the war, latterly as *Kommodore* of JG 6, with 40 kills to his credit.

13

Bf 109D (Wk-Nr 630) 'White N7' of Oberleutnant Johannes Steinhoff, *Staffelkapitän* of 10.(N)/JG 26, Jever, December 1939

One of the handful of semi-autonomous nightfighter *Staffeln*, nearly all of which used the same marking combination of an 'N' to the left of the fuselage cross and an individual number to the right (on both port and starboard sides), Steinhoff's *Dora* also displays two victory bars on the tailfin for the Wellingtons he claimed in the historic 18 December 'Battle of the German Bight'. 10.(N)/JG 26 was later incorporated into the nightfighter arm proper, but by that time 'Mäcki' Steinhoff was long gone, first to JG 52 and then JG 77. In December 1944 he was appointed *Kommodore* of the Me 262-equipped JG 7 before joining JV 44 early in 1945. He was badly injured on 18 April 1945, having added 174 more kills to the two seen here.

14

Bf 109E 'Red 5' of Leutnant Josef Buerschgens, 2./JG 26 'Schlageter', Odendorf, September 1939

It was in this standard early finish *Emil* that Josef Buerschgens scored the first of JG 26's more than 2700 aerial victories of the war, a French Curtiss Hawk H-75A of GC II/5 downed on 28 September 1939. He was himself severely injured in the encounter, however, and did not return to combat flying until towards the close of the French campaign. Between 9 June and the end of August 1940 he achieved nine more kills before being shot down near Rye – by the rear gunner of a Bf 110 – to sit out the rest of the hostilities as a PoW! Note, incidentally, the early style 2. *Staffel* 'Devil's Head' emblem compared to that on Losigkeit's machine (profile 11).

15

Bf 109E-4 'Double Chevron' of Hauptmann Wolfgang Lippert, *Gruppenkommandeur* II/JG 27, Montreuil, September 1940

Lippert's aircraft illustrates the general toning-down effect achieved by dappling the *hellblau* finish applied to the fuselage sides earlier in 1940. The *Gruppe* badge on the yellow cowling is the 'Berlin bear', indicative of II./JG 27's home town – for a long time the *Gruppe's* mobile ops room was a converted dou-ble-decker Berlin bus! Wolfgang Lippert led II./JG 27 in the Balkans and the opening months of the Russian campaign before deployment to the Western Desert, where he was lost on 23 November 1941 with his score at 25 (see *Aircraft of the Aces 2*).

16

Bf 109E-1 'Red 1' of Oberleutnant Gerd Framm, *Staffelkapitän* 2./JG 27, Krefeld, January 1940

The interest in Germany's former colonies shown by Hauptmann Helmut Riegel, the first *Gruppenkommandeur* of I./JG 27, is well known from his designing and introducing the famous negro and tiger's head 'Africa' badge. The pilots of his 2. *Staffel* went one better. They named each of their aircraft after one such colony, the *Staffelkapitän*, for example, opting for 'Samoa' (which was a lot easier for the *Staffel* painter to get on the cowling than the choice of another pilot: 'Deutsch-Südwest Afrika'!). Note too the *Kapitän's* aerial mast pennant and aft fuselage diagonal band. Framm would survive the war with ten victories.

17

Bf 109E-1 'Black Chevron' of Oberleutnant Josef Priller, *Gruppen-Adjutant* I./JG 51, Eutingen, September 1939

The first wartime machine of future *Experte* Josef Priller was a perfectly standard splinter-green *Emil* displaying a regulation set of markings plus *Gruppe* emblem. Note, however, the first sign of individuality – Priller's personal 'Ace of Hearts' emblem below the cockpit. This would accompany him when he began first his 12-month stint as *Staffelkapitän* of 6./JG 51 in October (see photo page 50), and then his climb to real fame with JG 26 (for details of Priller's later 'Ace of Hearts' *see Aircraft of the Aces 9*). 'Pips' Priller would end the war with 101 victories, one of the very few to achieve a century solely against the Allies in the west.

18

Bf 109E 'White 13' of Feldwebel Heinz Bär, 1./JG 51, Pihen, September 1940

Another future 'Great' who began his war with JG 51 was Heinz 'Pritzl' Bär. And just like Priller's 'Ace of Hearts', Bär too had his individual marking: the 'lucky' number 13, which adorned nearly every aircraft he flew in combat, from the early *Emils* such as that depicted here right up to, and including, the Me 262 jet (by which time the 8 victories sported by this 'White 13' would have grown to a final total of 220!). Note too the *Staffel* badge, yet another variation on the *Mickey Mouse* theme inspired by the *Condor Legion's* 3.J/88, this one brought back from Spain and devised by 1./JG 51's then *Kapitän* Oberleutnant Douglas Pitcairn.

19

Bf 109E 'Black 1' of Hauptmann Horst Tietzen, *Staffelkapitän* 5./JG 51, Marquise, August 1940

In contrast to Priller and Bär, the career of Horst 'Jakob' Tietzen – one of JG 51's first pair of Knight's Cross winners – was short-lived. He would add just 3 more victories to the 17 shown here on 15 August before being posted missing off the Kent coast 72 hours later. The *Gruppe* badge, which at this time was carried aft of the fuselage cross in place of a more normal II. *Gruppe* horizontal bar, dates back to the beginning of the war, and features another oft-used object of derision in early Luftwaffe heraldry, Prime Minister Neville Chamberlain's umbrella! Note also that *Staffelkapitäne* were beginning to drop the practice of advertising their presence in the air by means of aerial pennants.

20

Bf 109E 'Black Double Chevron' of Hauptmann Wolfgang Ewald, *Gruppenkommandeur* I./JG 52, Coquelles, September 1940

Another *Gruppe* which for a while displayed its emblem aft of the fuselage cross was I./JG 52, although exactly why the 'Running boar' badge was reduced in size and removed from its place of prominence on the engine cowling is uncertain - perhaps an edict from on high not to detract from the new *Geschwader* shield below the cockpit? Ewald scored just two victories in the west before being posted as *Kommandeur* to III./JG 3 on the eastern front, where he steadily added a further 75 kills to his tally. He was to spend many years in Soviet cap-tivity after being brought down by Russian Flak on 14 July 1943.

21
Bf 109E (Wk-Nr 3335) 'Red 1' of Leutnant Hans Berthel, 2./JG 52, Bonn-Hangelar, October 1939

Flying the Bf 109 throughout, JG 52 was the Luftwaffe's most successful *Jagdgeschwader* of the war, claiming some 11,000 victories in all! But during the early months there was little indication of the success to come. Hans Berthel scored I.*Gruppe*'s first kill (a French LeO.451) on 6 October 1939 in this overall *schwarzgrün* (black-green) *Emil*. In the next eleven months he made it to acedom with another five victories before, as *Gruppenadjutant*, he was downed over Kent on 'Battle of Britain Day', 15 September 1940 – claimed in the records by a No 41 Sqn Spitfire, but after losing his tail unit in an aerial collision according to his own account!

22
Bf 109E 'White 8' of Hauptmann Hans-Karl Mayer, *Gruppenkommandeur* I./JG 53 'Pik-As', Etaples, September 1940

When promoted *Kommandeur* of I./JG 53, Hans-Karl Mayer apparently took with him the machine he had previously flown as *Kapitän* of 1.*Staffel*, hence the 'White 8' rather than double chevron markings. The last 3 of the 29 victory bars on the rudder represent the trio of Hurricanes claimed by Mayer on the same 15 September that saw Hans Berthel (above) go down. Mayer himself would be reported missing over the Channel on 17 October, having added just two more to his score. Note that the liberal use of yellow identification markings has here conveniently obliterated the controversial 'red ring' (see profile 24).

23
Bf 109E 'Black Chevron-Triangle' of Hauptmann Werner Mölders, *Gruppenkommandeur* III./JG 53 'Pik-As', Trier-Euren, March 1940

Mayer's predecessor as *Kapitän* of 1./JG 53, a certain Werner Mölders, was promoted to the command of III.*Gruppe* on 3 October 1939. Exactly five months later to the day World War 2 acedom was achieved with the downing of a Morane MS.406 fighter of GC II/3 near Metz – a fact recorded by the fifth victory bar on the tailfin as shown here. After that the rest is history, culminating in the award of the Diamonds on 16 July 1941 as the first fighter pilot to top the century, only to be followed four months later by a tragic death in a flying accident while en route from Russia to attend the funeral of Ernst Udet.

24
Bf 109E 'Black Chevron-Triangle' of Hauptmann Harro Harder, *Gruppenkommandeur* of III./JG 53 'Pik-As', Villiaze/Guernsey, August 1940

The height of the Battle of Britain and Mölders' successor at the head of III./JG 53 is still flying an *Emil* very similar in appearance to the machine above, even down to the early style narrow-bordered fuselage cross (although the Swastika has now moved from the rudder hinge-line to the tailfin). The one glaring difference, however, is the red ring covering the *Geschwader*'s famous 'Ace-of-Spades' badge, a sign of the *Reichsmarschall*'s disapproval of JG 53's present *Kommodore* (see text). The six victory bars depicted here relate to Harro Harder's success with a previous unit. He would claim five more – all Spitfires – in just forty-eight hours before being reported missing east of the Isle of Wight on 12 August – he

was shot down by No 609 Sqn ace Plt Off D M Crook (see *Aircraft of the Aces 12*).

25
Bf 109E-3 (Wk-Nr 1244) 'White 5' of Unteroffizier Stefan Litjens, 4./JG 53 'Pik-As', Mannheim-Sandhofen, October 1939

'Steff' Litjens' E-3 displays one of the many segmented camouflage schemes with which JG 53 experimented in the autumn of 1939. He claimed his first victory on 7 April 1940, and his score had risen to seven by the time the *Geschwader* left the Channel front. Despite losing the sight of one eye in Russia, he returned to combat over the Mediterranean and in homeland defence duties before an injury to his remaining eye finally forced his retirement from operational service in 1944 with a total of 38 victories.

26
Bf 109E 'White 1' of Oberleutnant Wolf-Dietrich Wilcke, *Staffelkapitän* 7./JG 53 'Pik-As', Wiesbaden-Erbenheim, October 1939

This *Emil* of Wilcke's bears the even more sharply defined splinter camouflage scheme which was to be found on many III.*Gruppe* aircraft during this period. Note, however, the early style narrow-bordered cross, albeit of the new larger size, combined with the Swastika centered on the rudder hinge-line. Like Mölders, 'Fürst' Wilcke also spent some time in French captivity. Shortly after his release he was promoted to *Kommandeur* of III.*Gruppe*, which he led in the Battle of Britain, over the Mediterranean and in Russia. Appointed *Kommodore* of JG 3, he was killed in action against USAAF P-51 Mustangs in March 1944, having amassed a total of 162 victories.

27
Bf 109E-4 'White 1' of Oberleutnant Hans Philipp, *Staffelkapitän* 4./JG 54, Hermelingen, October 1940

Like JG 52 based alongside them in the Pas de Calais, JG 54 are perhaps more famous for their later exploits on the eastern front. They did, however, contribute four names to the list of early Knight's Cross winners, among them Oberleutnant Hans Philipp, who had opened his score during II./JG 54's days in Poland (as I./JG 76). Here, his heavily mottled *Emil* displays 18 victory bars – the last 3 all No 66 Sqn Spitfires claimed on 13 October – as Philipp begins the long climb to the 206 victories he would ultimately achieve before he, too, fell to US fighters in the Battle of the *Reich*. Note the deep yellow of the recognition markings and the *Gruppe* badge featuring the 'Lion of Aspern', a reference to the unit's Austrian ancestry.

28
Bf 109E-4 (Wk-Nr 1572) 'Black 3' of Leutnant Erwin Leykauf, 8./JG 54, Guines-South, September 1940

References differ as to whether the five victories depicted here were scored by Leykauf during the Battle of France or the Battle of Britain. The latter would seem the more likely as II.*Gruppe* (the ex-I./JG 21) did not begin relocating their individual aircraft numbers from immediately aft of the cowling to the standard position ahead of the fuselage cross until mid-1940. Note the absence of the *Gruppe* badge (reputedly only carried by *Stab* machines), each *Staffel* displaying instead an emblem

THE APPENDICES

– in 8./JG 54's case the 'Piepmatz' (Cheeky sparrow) adorning the yellow cowling. Leykauf later served as *Gruppen-Adjutant* in Russia, where he was to achieve a further 28 kills.

29

Bf 109E-1 (Wk-Nr 4072) 'Red 1' of Hauptmann Hannes Trautloft, *Staffelkapitän* 2./JG 77, Juliusburg, September 1939

Before assuming command of I./JG 20 (see profile 9), Hannes Trautloft headed 2./JG 77 in Poland, where he scored the first of his 53 wartime kills (plus 4 in Spain). The red spinner and aft fuselage bands are presumably *Kapitän* identification markings (in the relevant *Staffel* colour) while the small red circle may refer back to I./JG 77's previous identity as IV./JG 132. Otherwise the *Emil* bears standard autumn 1939 camouflage and markings. The 'Tattered boot' emblem was introduced by *Gruppenkommandeur* Hauptmann Johannes Janke, who also gave the *Gruppe* its unofficial title of *'Wanderzirkus* Janke' – 'Janke's Travelling Circus'!

30

Bf 109E 'Black 1' of Feldwebel Robert Menge, 5./JG 77, Aalborg, August 1940

The most successful pilot of the Norwegian campaign, Menge's aircraft – like most II./JG 77 machines of this period – has had its 1940-style *hellblau* finish heavily oversprayed (carefully going round all markings and insignia). Note the *Gruppe* badge ahead of the cockpit. It was in this *Emil* that Menge claimed four Blenheim IVs lost during the disastrous Aalborg raid of 13 August. Later transferred to JG 26, Menge often flew as *Geschwaderkommodore* Adolf Galland's wingman. He was killed while taking off from Marquise on 14 June 1941, his final score of 18 including 4 gained with the *Condor Legion* in Spain.

31

Bf 109E 'Yellow 1' of Oberleutnant Wilhelm Moritz, *Staffelkapitän* 6./JG 77, Kristiansand-Kjevik, September 1940

Another II.*Gruppe* machine illustrating the additional dapple applied to the *hellblau* fuselage sides and vertical tail surfaces - this time with traces of the original aircraft identity code (NI + ZW) still showing through. Moritz, an ex-*Zerstörer* pilot, did not score while with JG 77, and in January 1941 was posted to a training unit. His time was to come, however, for after serving both in Defence of the *Reich* and in Russia, Wilhelm Moritz became one of the leading exponents of the *Sturm* tactics against US heavy bombers, ending the war with at least 44 kills (see *Aircraft of the Aces 9*).

32

Bf 109E 'Yellow 11' of Feldwebel Alfred Held, 6./JG 77, Nordholz, September 1939

This otherwise unremarkable early *Emil* is reportedly the first German fighter to shoot down an RAF aircraft in World War 2 (a Wellington on 4 September). Bearing standard autumn 1939 camouflage and markings, it also displays II./JG 77's early *Gruppe* badge of a 'stylised seagull' (compare to the later version worn on the two aircraft above). But the all-important item is that single victory bar which would adorn the tailfin for less than a fortnight, for Alfred Held was killed in a flying accident in this *Emil* at Nordholz on 17 September 1939.

33

Bf 109E (Wk-Nr 1279) 'Yellow 5' of Feldwebel Hans Troitzsch, 6./JG 77, Wangerooge, December 1939

Unlike Held, the other contender for the first victory of 4 September survived to participate in the 18 December Battle of the German Bight as well, hence the three victory bars on the tailfin of Troitzsch's Wk-Nr 1279. The changes to II./JG 77's aircraft between the two engagements are obvious – most apparent is the freshly applied coat of *hellblau* to the fuselage sides and tail, plus the new size and style of the fuselage cross and repositioning of the Swastika. But note too not only the new *Gruppe* badge, but also the *Staffel* emblem on the rudder introduced by *Kapitän* Franz-Heinz Lange.

34

Bf 109D 'White Chevron-Triangle' of Hauptmann Hannes Gentzen, *Jagdgruppe* 102 (I./ZG 2), Bernburg, October 1939

As the *Dora* of the only Bf 109 ace of the Polish campaign, this aircraft displays seven victory bars as evidence. Also visible is the *Gruppe*'s 'Hunter of Bernburg' badge below the windscreen. But it is not certain whether the unofficial 'Black Hand Gang' emblem on the nose was worn in Poland or applied prior to JG.102's western front deployment. There Gentzen was to achieve just two more kills – his eighth on the Bf 109D and the ninth and last after the *Gruppe*'s re-equipment with the twin-engined Bf 110, the aircraft in which he was killed whilst performing a scramble take off from Neufchateau on 26 May 1940.

35

Bf 109E 'Yellow 13' of Feldwebel Kurt Ubben, 6.(J)/TrGr.186, Wangerooge, March 1940

One of the most conspicuous of all early Bf 109 *Staffel* markings adorned the *Emils* of 6.(J)/TrGr.186, part of the *Jagdgruppe* initially intended for service aboard the never-to-be-completed aircraft carrier *Graf Zeppelin*. Although the *Staffel* missed out on the Battle of the German Bight, the pilot of 'Yellow 13' was an *Experte* in the making. 'Kuddel' Ubben scored his first kill – a Fokker D-XXI over De Kooy – on the opening day of the campaign in the west. Thereafter he rose through the ranks of JG 77 in Russia and the Mediterranean until promoted to *Kommodore* of JG 2 'Richthofen'. With a final total of 110 victories, he was killed in action against P-47s over France on 27 April 1944.

36

Bf 109E 'Black 1' of Oberleutnant Herbert Ihlefeld, *Gruppenkommandeur* I.(J)/LG 2, Marquise, September 1940

Presumably the aircraft he had previously flown as *Staffelkapitän* of 2.(J)/LG 2, Ihlefeld's Bf 109 shows some slight variations in its yellow tactical recognition markings, namely the odd scalloped effect immediately ahead of the cockpit and the painting of only the rear section of the rudder. 2.*Staffel*'s 'Top hat' badge still appears aft of the fuselage cross. Already a 7-victory *Condor Legion* ace, Ihlefeld scored over 20 kills during the Battle of Britain before going on to even greater things. He commanded various *Geschwader*, finally ending the war at the head of JG 1 with 123 victories to his credit.

95

FIGURE PLATES

1

Seen here sporting the Oak Leaves to his Knight's Cross, awarded on 21 September for his 40th victory, Major Werner Mölders is wearing standard officer's service dress of tunic and breeches, together with the *Schirmmütze* (officer's peaked cap) and *Pelzstiefeln* (flying boots). Note too the woollen inner gloves. The only non-regulation item is the sheepskin jacket, shown open to display the ribbon of the Iron Cross, Second Class, in the top button, the Iron Cross, First Class, on the left breast pocket and the pilot's badge below. Also just visible are the major's collar patches.

2

Major Adolf Galland's badges of rank – on his collar and epaulettes – are seen here to better advantage. Note, how-ever, the reversed positions of his pilot's badge and Iron Cross, First Class (and the absence of the Second Class ribbon). Although wearing basically the same outfit as Mölders, Galland presents an entirely different appearance by having adorned his bottom half with a cut down ex-RAF Irvin flying suit that he so often favoured on operations during this period. Also in evi-dence, as always, are the two Galland trademarks – the bat-tered peak cap and cigar!

3

Hauptmann Günther Lützow rings the changes completely in his summer combination flying suit (Model K So/34) with its multitude of zippered pockets worn with the officer's gabar-dine *Feldmütze* field service forage cap – more colloquially known as a *Schiffchen* ('little ship'). Note too the officer's pat-tern belt and holster (the latter housing any one of the various small 7.65 mm automatics which were issued to aircrew), the cloth sleeve patch denoting Lützow's rank and his Knight's Cross awarded on 18 September 1940 after he had achieved 15 aerial victories.

4

Hauptmann Helmut Wick in typically enthusiastic pose, describing a recent encounter, while at the same time manag-ing to hide all traces of rank badges and decorations. It may be noted, however, that he is wearing the alternative style of ser-vice dress tunic with patch pockets and the *JAGDGESCHWADER RICHTHOFEN* cuff titling on his right sleeve. The impression of his just having returned from a cross-Channel sortie is further heightened by the leather flying helmet and microphone lead, the early-style kapok segmented life-jacket and the map stuffed into his left flying boot.

5

In contrast to Wick, Hauptmann Heinz Bretnütz is wearing the later-style inflatable life-jacket and mouth-piece on the left breast and compressed-air cylinder at the waist. Further proof of the overwater nature of the Bf 109 pilot's operations in the late summer of 1940 is graphically provided by the high-visibil-ity yellow helmet cover sported by Bretnütz and – of more practical use in the event of an enforced ditching in the Channel – the flare cartridges bandoliered about his left flying boot, the shorter (83 mm) ones being single starburst flares and the longer (135 mm) models containing double stars. Both versions were visible at a distance of some 2.5 km under rea-sonably good conditions, and burned for about six seconds.

6

Hauptmann Hermann-Friedrich Joppien displays one last vari-ety on an already familiar theme by opting for winter flying suit trousers (with button pockets), combined with a privately pur-chased leather zippered jacket with fur collar. Such jackets were a popular item with many *Jagdwaffe* pilots, and were to be found in a wide range of styles and patterns either with or without badges of rank, decorations and epaulettes attached as shown here. Note that although each of the figures depicted on these pages is wearing the same style of footwear, namely the *Pelzstiefel*, the choice of gloves was apparently a matter of personal preference.

INDEX